"In a culture that is hurting and ̲ ̲ ̲ ̲ ̲ing healing, this book offers a much-needed message of hope. Through a compassionate and integrated approach, Brya Hanan provides practical strategies, stories of resilience, and evidence-based insights. This book is a must-have resource for anyone on a healing journey."

Julia Marie Hogan-Werner
Therapist and author

"Hanan continues to offer the most holy, healing work in her office, on Catholic social media, and now in this book. We are all so lucky to get to learn from her and be invited to see in a new way how God desires to heal us from within."

Erica Tighe Campbell
Author of *Living the Seasons* and creator of Be A Heart

"Hanan does an incredible job diving into what can seem like rough territory by Christian standards. She artfully expresses the importance and meaning behind inner child work while upholding the value and dignity of the whole person, body, and soul. Utilizing anecdotal as well as research-based evidence, she demonstrates the power of becoming like little children again and healing wounds we often never knew existed. Her personal examples also help immensely as she combines her own Catholic experience with that of her work with clients."

Lisa Gormley
Wife, mother, and Catholic therapist

"Hanan has written a much-needed book on healing, blending Catholic teaching with psychological research. This book is written with a tender, compassionate voice from someone personally walking the journey of healing and walking alongside those in the healing process in her therapy practice. I can't say enough about the practical exercises and prayer experiences at the end of each chapter. They are valuable tools and gifts for healing, no matter where you are on your journey."

Michelle Benzinger
Abiding Together podcast cohost, creative director, and speaker

"Hanan takes you on a personal journey that is fresh, enlightening, and impactful. She tenderly weaves clinical knowledge with scripture and relatable examples that would benefit anyone looking to grow deeper in their faith and sense of self-worth. This will help many, and I will recommend it to many!"

Regina Boyd
Therapist and author of *Leaving Loneliness Behind*

"This book is gold! Hanan has written a treasure that will transform hearts and souls for generations to come. I read this and read my own story, my loved ones' stories, and my clients' stories. It feels like a missing piece of the puzzle has been found. Healing is no longer complex and abstract but attainable and practical. I will not only continue referencing this book for my own personal growth but will be passing it out to all of my clients as well. What a gift!"

Melissa Tablada
Catholic psychotherapist

"Jesus said we must become like trusting little children to enter the kingdom of heaven. For most of us, learning to trust like that seems nearly impossible. Our wounds and self-protections make it extremely difficult for us to trust anyone, including God. In *Befriending Your Inner Child*, Hanan gives us a tried-and-true path to finding inner peace and wholeness in Christ. Drawing upon her years of experience as a therapist and her own healing from childhood trauma, Hanan writes with refreshing clarity and wisdom. I loved every chapter and gleaned many valuable insights as I read through it. I have already recommended it to several people. I strongly encourage you to not only read through it but, in the process, to discover and befriend your beloved inner child, buried beneath all the ways you have learned to survive."

Bob Schuchts
Author of *Be Healed*

Befriending your *Inner Child*

A Catholic Approach to Healing and Wholeness

Brya Hanan

AVE MARIA PRESS AVE Notre Dame, Indiana

© 2024 by Brya Hanan

All rights reserved. No part of this book may be used or reproduced in any manner whatsoever, except in the case of reprints in the context of reviews, without written permission from Ave Maria Press®, Inc., P.O. Box 428, Notre Dame, IN 46556, 1-800-282-1865.

Founded in 1865, Ave Maria Press is a ministry of the United States Province of Holy Cross.

www.avemariapress.com

Paperback: ISBN-13 978-1-64680-304-0

E-book: ISBN-13 978-1-64680-305-7

Cover image © gettyimages.com.

Cover design by Kristen Hornyak Bonelli.

Text design by Christopher D. Tobin.

Printed and bound in the United States of America.

Library of Congress Cataloging-in-Publication Data is available.

To my family past, present, and future, and to
all the clients I have had the privilege of accompanying.
Here's to creating a legacy of healing.

Contents

Introduction

I know a devout laywoman who goes to Mass Monday through Sunday. She reads her daily devotions, prays the Rosary at night, and proclaims the goodness of God in every conversation, and yet, when she is alone with her thoughts, she has an aching sense that she is not good enough. She must do more. Be more. Try harder.

I know an electrician who adores his family. He is proud of his ability to provide for them and works tirelessly to be the kind of man he never experienced in childhood, but when he feels stressed, he yells at the top of his lungs at his children and then retreats by locking himself in his office and scrolling on his phone for hours.

I know a successful life coach who can motivate and inspire others with her encouraging words and enlightening posts on Instagram. She can speak on podcasts about the value of spiritual freedom and give inspirational talks to a crowd. Yet, when she returns home to visit her mother, she feels seven years old again. She quietly takes in her mother's condescending remarks and works hard not to do or say anything that will "set her mother off."

I know a devoted stay-at-home mom who is loved by many in her community. She lives a sacramental life, introduces her children to various saints, and has them partake in many different religious activities. She ends her day with family prayer and then tucks her little ones in bed. Yet, the same mother building the domestic church often describes herself as a "ticking time bomb." She stuffs her feelings down day after day, just as she did when she was teenager, and then passive-aggressively makes hurtful comments to her husband when he returns home from work and gossips with her friends.

I begin with these stories from clients I have worked with because all of these stories represent me, and they represent you too. We are all interiorly divided and can feel at war within our own selves.

We can identify our strengths, desires, and hopes and yet still feel pulled into old patterns, childish behavior, stark feelings, and immature thoughts that seem at odds with who we want to be. Our lives can echo the words of St. Paul when he says, "I do not understand my own actions. For I do not do what I want, but I do the very thing I hate" (Rom 7:15). Despite our best efforts, there seems to be a never-ending tension as we strive to live out our God-given dignity in every aspect of our life. It is from this place of tension that we struggle to be who God created us to be.

When I started to identify my own internal division, I had no idea what to do with these parts of myself or even how to articulate them to others. In fact, I did not have the language of "parts." I simply believed what I was noticing within me was the sum of who I am, which led me to the conclusion that I will never be enough.

My feelings of inadequacy became the driving force in my life and forerunner in all of my relationships, including the relationship I had with God. As a result, I worked hard to prove my worthiness. When I entered graduate school and began studying counseling psychology, I then quite naturally sought the answers as to why I felt so inadequate in psychological theory. However, learning about psychology didn't take the conflict within me away either. In fact, the war within me only intensified. There was no class, counseling theory, book, or case conceptualization that seemed to provide what my body and soul needed. I still felt the same.

Without knowing how to apply what I was learning, these conflicting pieces of myself continued to rise to the surface, and as they did, I felt incongruous and lacking in integrity. I did not know what I truly wanted or felt. More often than not, all I could experience was shame and paralyzing confusion that kept me far from the truth of who God says I am.

That is, until I discovered my inner child. When I began to see the child within me, who is so worthy of love and compassion, and began to befriend her, the inadequacy and accompanying shame lifted. I could see the truth again: I am enough, I am loved, and I am God's child. The conflicting thoughts and feelings within me were not proof of my inadequacy but a reflection of my inner child who is fearfully and wonderfully made (see Psalms 139:14), and also deeply wounded and in need of healing.

As I allowed this truth to settle into my entire being, the shroud of darkness and confusion began to dissipate, and instead of experiencing divisiveness, I began experiencing wholeness. I was no longer afraid, frustrated, or confused about what I held within me. Instead, for the first time, I had an insatiable desire to enter into the depths of my internal fracture with compassion. I felt committed to love and care for my inner poverty- the child within who had little resources to cope with big emotions, little vocabulary to understand her experiences, and who had been deprived of acknowledgment and deep attunement.

This is where this book comes in. It is my sincere hope to share with you what I learned along the way so that you, too, can reclaim the truth of who you are and allow that truth to settle into your entire being so you can love and be loved well. If you are feeling a little ambivalent and cautious about this work, I welcome your feelings. I was also ambivalent and cautious when I started learning about my inner child and "inner child work." Inner child work has been sensationalized by secular media and adopted in many new-age practices that can feel far from Catholic theology and Christian tradition. Many therapists have also struggled to delve into the full power of this work due to the limited resources and training that are available, leaving the exploration of the concept of one's inner child futile. But as someone who integrates inner child work into my daily living and who is a devoted follower of Christ, I can assure you that when we harmonize the work with our faith, it becomes a transforming invitation to enter the depths of our interior world and God's expansive love for us.

As we embark on this healing journey, we have an opportunity to participate in God's healing work and to live as God's children. We do this by loving ourselves the way God loves us and bringing our inner child closer to Jesus. Jesus says, "Let the children come to me, and do not hinder them; for to such belongs the kingdom of God" (Lk 18:16), and throughout this journey, we will learn how to follow this command in a way that integrates our body and soul and honors where we are at and what we are feeling.

Without a secure and robust understanding of ourselves and the language and tools to be a good friend to our inner child, we risk allowing our child parts to rule our adult lives, which is often responsible for the chaos, dysfunction, emotional distress, physical illness, spiritual dryness, and despair we face. In the words of Dr. David Richo in his book *How to Be an Adult*, "The untreated traumas of childhood become the frustrating dramas of adulthood" (Richo, 14). Our past invades our present, and we become the person we are created to be and the perfect love we were fashioned for, the perfect love that binds our wounds (see Psalms 147:3). Instead of living from our belovedness, we will live from our woundedness, and as a result, we will be disconnected from the child within us who longs to be loved and healed.

Consider the people mentioned at the beginning of this introduction. The laywoman is disconnected from the child within her who has learned from a very young age that she will never be able to make people happy. There's always something she is doing wrong and needs to improve to earn love. This belief has transferred to her relationship with God. The electrician is disconnected from the child within who feels powerless and never learned how to regulate his emotions. His and others' emotions often felt scary, so now when faced with them he lashes out in desperation and ignorance, then retreats in guilt and shame. The successful life coach is disconnected from the child within who longs for her mother's approval and has learned to do everything in her power to stay on her good side and avoid rejection. The stay-at-home mom is disconnected from the child within her who has never learned how to communicate her needs. Her needs are "selfish," so she adapts by silencing them and projecting her inner anger onto others.

As imperfect humans, we often operate from our deepest wounds instead of God's expansive love. This is because when faced with our wounds, we have not learned how to receive God's compassion and extend it to the parts of us that need it the most. We have not learned to see the child within us and offer that child what they needed all along. We may have learned how to cope, survive, and "keep going," but healing work is much more than that. Therefore, to experience true healing, we must tap into our inner child's wounds and the emotions, feelings, and self-protections connected to them and befriend them just as God does.

In order to accomplish this important healing work throughout our journey together, we will be relying on the wisdom of the Holy Spirit and Holy Mother Church and the wisdom of Psychology and Neurobiology to aid in our understanding. We must keep in mind that in this work of achieving wholeness and healing, on this side of heaven, there will always be new things to learn, grow, heal, and bring into integration. We might never know ourselves or all the truths within the sciences and theology completely. We might never see every wound healed or achieve perfect wholeness here on earth, and that's okay. St. Paul writes in his First Letter to the Corinthians, "Now I know in part; then I shall understand fully, even as I have been fully understood" (13:12). St. Paul reveals that despite our best efforts, there will always be truth that will remain a mystery and parts of us that we may not completely understand, but we can take comfort in knowing that God does know the truth. God does know us fully and has created us to be whole and will restore our wholeness completely in heaven. Therefore, we can trust in God as we venture into the child inside of us and rely on his grace to carry us through. When truth eludes us and our minds and bodies reach their limitation, we can find and develop our security in God to mend and fill every gap.

What You Can Expect from This Book

In part 1, we will explore why reclaiming our inner child is important and why it is the heart of healing work. We will also explore our disintegration, the competing thoughts and feelings we hold within, more thoroughly, including the different parts of our inner child and why befriending these parts is necessary.

In part 2, we will explore how to experience healing and wholeness by examining the five *A*'s of befriending our inner child: *anchor*, *acknowledge*, *attune*, *ask*, and *act*. As a result, we will be given the opportunity to:

1. Encounter our authentic core and reclaim him or her as the beloved.

2. Be honest about our emotional, physical, and spiritual ailments and the wounds they are connected to and practice self-compassion.

3. Identify the ways we have learned to protect ourselves from further wounding and make new commitments to better care for ourselves and protect ourselves more virtuously.

4. Develop greater safety and security in our bodies and experience God's reparenting.

5. Learn how to be Spirit-led adults and support what is fractured within us, becoming more one with God in the process.

Each chapter will include stories of clients who have befriended their inner child and who are experiencing these five outcomes. Names of clients and some details have been changed to protect their identities, but their stories are very real. You will find opportunities to connect with their stories and my own story, as well as opportunities to pray, complete "befriending work," and participate in guided meditations in part 1. Recorded by me, the guided meditations are invitations to further discover your inner child and experience who they are and how they show up in your body. Please scan the qr code here or go to avemariapress.com/befriending-inner-child-meditations to listen to meditations for chapters 1–5. The befriending work is an opportunity to apply the content and practice befriending your own inner child.

As you engage with this book, it is important to read at a gentle and slow pace, and continuously check in with yourself. If you find yourself becoming dysregulated (heart begins to race, you feel hot or sweaty, increasingly agitated, have suicidal thoughts, or are on the verge of an emotional breakdown), I encourage you to pause, regulate yourself, and seek support. This is not a book to rush through and use to bypass your feelings. It is meant to be experiential, relational, and responsive to whatever comes up for you. So I encourage you to honor your body and the emotions that arise, notice what is happening within you as you read, and take breaks and deep breaths. Also, consider journaling your thoughts, feelings, inspirations, and reactions or processing these with someone safe, sharing what stands out to you in the book.

We are about to begin a journey that many of us have never dared to embark on, a journey that will not be easy. This journey requires your presence, honesty, courage, and vulnerability. We may feel uncomfortable feelings, uncover distressing thoughts and beliefs, and remember many painful memories we wish we could just forget. We may experience profound grief for what our inner child may have lost and never received in childhood. We may have to acknowledge trauma and subsequent wounds that we haven't thought about in years. We may have to confront the complexity of our stories and the complexity of the stories from the generations that came before us. We may have to take a hard look at parts of ourselves that feel much easier to bury in the recesses of our mind.

As challenging as the journey ahead may be, if you come with an open mind and heart and make room for your inner child, you will experience a kind of joy, hope, safety, and security that you never knew could be possible. You will rediscover the joy of being alive and who you truly are at your core: a person who is created for boundless love, healing, and wholeness.

You will learn how to befriend your inner child and, in turn, embrace and live out your identity as God's beloved child from here on out.

Part 1

Discovering Your Inner Child

/

Becoming One

I entered the same dreary therapy room, approached the same desolate couch, and prepared to discuss the same debilitating problems. During this time in my healing journey, going to therapy felt wildly repetitive. I would show up week after week, but deep within, I remained hopeless. No matter how often I poured my heart out, explored my trauma, admitted my weaknesses, and developed new coping skills and insight, I still felt so wounded.

As I sat face-to-face with my therapist, I pondered giving up and telling her this would be my last session. My therapist looked at me with eyes full of compassion and gently nodded in recognition as if she knew exactly what I was thinking. Afraid to let my hopelessness be seen, I quickly turned my gaze away from her. She then asked me, "How are you doing?" It was a question she usually led with and a question I normally answered with some kind of platitude and awkward smile, but this time was different. I felt unhinged, with no protective barriers left to conceal my despair.

I let out a big sigh and allowed myself to be completely raw and honest. "Not good," I said. "I am tired of feeling so broken." My eyes quickly flooded with tears as I heard the truth leave my lips. There was no way my despair could go unnoticed. I had allowed myself to be fully seen in my pain. A few seconds of silence passed as we sat with the weight of what I had just uttered. My therapist nodded her head again, validating my words. She then responded, "I can only imagine. You have been working so hard to heal."

3

Tears began to run down my cheeks in recognition of the validity of her words. She was right. I had been working so hard to heal. I was reading all the mental health and spiritual books I could access. I went to daily Mass and Eucharistic Adoration, prayed throughout the day, and attended Bible studies, retreats, and conferences. I was journaling my feelings and writing papers on my life experiences. I was meeting with a spiritual director on top of meeting with my therapist. I was doing the work, so why was I feeling so unhealed?

I then voiced my frustration and the fear underneath my words that it would always be this way. My therapist seemed to see something I hadn't. She retorted, "Is that how you felt as a child?" My eyes grew wide. I hadn't thought of my child self in years. Suddenly, a memory resurfaced in my mind that caught me by surprise.

I entered the memory with curiosity and became a bystander in my ten-year-old self's bedroom. It was there that I saw my child self sitting on my flowery twin-sized bed, looking at a calendar. On the calendar was a series of scribbled sad faces. I had drawn these sad faces to document how I felt.

Growing up, I was plagued by a pervasive feeling of inadequacy. Unfortunately, at the tender age of four, I became severely wounded. I was sexually abused by my grandfather, which led to high stress and conflict between my immediate and extended family that I had felt responsible for. In response to the abuse, I became more curious and confused about my body, which only left me feeling an incredible amount of shame.

The shame intensified when my strong-willed and outgoing personality often got me in trouble at home. I wondered if I was just too much for my parents, and since my biological father was out of the picture for as long as I could remember, I often wondered if I was just too much for him too.

This shame and internalized belief that "I am too much" carried with me into school, and it impeded my ability to excel academically. Under the weight of it all, I was left feeling stunted, slow, and stupid. Extracurriculars were no exception. When I was put into dance and soccer, I was clumsy and shy. I found myself struggling to keep up with the other girls or passively moving to evade being seen. And when I looked in the mirror, my thick curly hair, darker skin tone, unibrow, and fuzzy arms and legs left me feeling like an outcast compared to others. Needless to say, I struggled to feel good enough.

As I watched the scene unfold, I saw myself draw another sad face with tearful eyes. My heart sank in recognizing this little girl and how hopeless she felt. I could feel her in my body—her deep sadness and choking fear that nothing would ever change.

For my child self, the calendar confirmed that no matter what she did, nothing ever took the sad feelings away. Each day she still felt them. She could try to do everything "right" and try to change herself to feel more worthy, and she would still be left in despair. As I sat in my adult body holding the weight of this painful memory, I realized that what I was experiencing in my adult life wasn't just my adult self's experiences. My child self's wounds and how she tried to cope had resurfaced.

I was actually feeling her feelings and dealing with those feelings now in the same way I had as a little girl. My adult experiences were triggering her painful wounds that never healed and her unmet needs that were never tended to. As I made these connections, for the first time in my life, I remembered an abandoned part of myself and was attuned to her experience, and as I did, this sad little girl was no longer buried in the tombstone of my past. She became alive, and I knew she needed my care and attention.

I don't know how the session ended. Nothing other than my child self and this memory seemed to matter, but from that moment on, my healing journey and how I saw myself was never the same. I began the work of befriending my inner child.

The True Nature of Healing Work

Healing work is not about eradicating our distressing feelings or our painful past; healing work is about making space for our experiences, both past and present, and discovering the hidden parts or subpersonalities of ourselves that have not experienced

God's tender mercy. It is the work of befriending our inner child and living as God's whole child—mind, body, and soul.

So often, when doing healing work, we try to erase our inner child. Usually this happens at the unconscious and subconscious level. This is nothing we do deliberately. We simply are not aware and compassionate toward the immature, pestering, reactive, and emotional parts we discover within ourselves.

In our desperation for healing, we do everything in our power to no longer feel our inner child—their pain, worry, sadness, anger, powerlessness, fear, loneliness, and restlessness. We might even engage in good things, such as going to therapy, reading books, attending retreats, and receiving the sacraments, in order to no longer hear their cries. Perhaps that is why you have chosen to read this book. Maybe part of you hopes you will finally be free from those little voices inside of you who never seem satisfied, who remind you of painful experiences, who are quick to defend and react, and who seem to demand more and more attention.

It makes sense that we would work so hard to erase our inner child, or that when we are faced with our wounds and fragility, we would try to disconnect from them. It is just too painful to sit with our imperfection. We want complete healing now. We desire it more than anything, and this desire is valid. It's what God desires for us too. Complete healing and restoration are our eternal reward, but unfortunately, on this side of heaven, no book will silence those small and vulnerable voices for good. Nor will the most transformative retreat, informative conference, or powerful therapy session. Our fragmented inner child is here to stay. But before you put this book down and become discouraged, I will tell you why this is good news.

In my enlightening therapy session, I realized the internal divide within myself that I was desperate to fix was not just caused by the painful experiences in my life that I needed to heal from or solely the result of sin that I needed to repent and release. The internal divide within myself—this persistent shame, sadness, and hopelessness I felt—was a part of my inner child. In the deepest corners of my heart, there lived a sad little girl who just wanted to feel as if she was enough. Trying to rationalize my wounds and no longer experience the distress that came with them was an attempt to eliminate a very important and necessary part of myself.

Therefore, we need our distress and painful experiences to help us see the child within and the forgotten truths that form our present understanding of who we are. As we enter into a relationship with our inner child, we draw near to their feelings, thoughts, memories, wounds, dreams, hopes, passions, defenses, vows, and agreements, and we discover a way to love and support them, hand in hand with God. It is in the context of relationship—relationship with God, with our inner child, and with others—that we no longer abandon ourselves but instead allow ourselves to experience God's healing and wholeness.

From Self-Abandonment to Self-Compassion

Unfortunately, many of us have no idea what it means to befriend our inner child and no longer abandon ourselves. We resist our inner child and the valuable information that this child holds. We reject their cries and even protests and often project or transmit their pain onto others. It is as if we are constantly on the run from our own selves.

Psychological self-abandonment is very different from the Christian view of self-abandonment or self-denial. In the Christian worldview, self-abandonment or self-denial is when we accept trials and suffering and surrender our natural consolations and disordered attachments to God's providence and care. It is about drawing closer to God and becoming more dependent on God in the process, but in the psychological sense, self-abandonment only brings us further away from self, God, and others.

In psychological self-abandonment, we abandon ourselves and become fragmented because, from an early age, we have learned to reject our thoughts, feelings, and needs out of fear and survival. It's how we have learned to manage our pain. Instead of allowing ourselves to feel our pain and share it in our relationships with others, we neglect our pain and find ways to distract ourselves from our inner world. This distraction could be anything from going to daily Mass to scrolling on our phones for hours. It doesn't matter if the distraction is holy or helpful. If what we use to distract ourselves doesn't reach the heart of what we are severed from, we won't feel our inner child's hurt. Our inner child will remain untouched, unseen, and uncared for.

In her book *The Journey from Abandonment to Healing*, psychotherapist Susan Anderson writes, "Abandonment is our first fear. It is a primal fear—a fear universal to the human experience. As infants, we lay screaming in our cribs, terrified that when our mothers left the room, they were never coming back. Abandonment is a fear that we will be left alone forever with no one to protect us, to see to our most urgent needs" (Anderson, 9). This fear permeates many of our actions. We all long to be seen, to be heard, to be known, and to be loved. When we live with a fear that our most urgent needs won't be met, we feel abandoned. Something withers and decays inside of us. Our true self begins a slow death, and if something is dead, we bury it, and our inner child is no exception.

When we are estranged from our inner child, we struggle to be secure adults who feel equipped to befriend what we see and experience in the present. Without consistent experiences of care, protection, and pursuit in early childhood, it becomes second nature to avoid protecting and pursuing what is sad, lonely, anxious, fearful, scared, or angry within us as adults. We begin to mirror our caregivers in how we show up with ourselves. I see this all the time in my work as a therapist. When we peel back the layers of a client's self-abandonment and explore their early childhood experiences, we always find a caregiver who was too busy for their child's emotional world; a caregiver who was too traumatized or preoccupied with their own struggles to emotionally care for their child; or a caregiver who did not have the skills or capacity to attune to them and therefore quickly dismissed them, minimized their pain, or tried to provide a quick fix.

We can also think we are practicing spiritual self-abandonment when in reality it is psychological self-abandonment. We may offer up our feelings too quickly. We may pray that the

Lord will take away our woundedness without ever taking the time to process our feelings. We may focus our attention on the positive or immediately "offer up" our distressing emotions to make our suffering feel more redemptive without exploring what these distressing emotions are trying to communicate to us. Although these actions can be virtuous and, when rooted in love, a powerful act of faith, many of us have bypassed our inner child and have used spirituality as a way to dismiss our feelings. But as I continue integrating this healing work in my spiritual life and accompany others in my work as a therapist, I discover time and time again that even our most virtuous actions won't be fruitful if we have ignored our wounds and pain and have abandoned ourselves.

And that's what makes our wounds, wounds. We are not wounded because we have experienced difficult experiences and trauma, but because after we experienced something that made us question whether we are loved or safe, we were alone with those questions. Nobody could help us see the truth and show up in a way that helped us feel whole. Instead, after our most painful and scariest experiences, we were abandoned in our darkest hour. In the absence of tender compassion, we were left with a harrowing belief that maybe we are all alone. Maybe, just maybe, nobody will hear our cries and come for us.

It is from this place of deep abandonment that we become psychologically fractured. Dan Siegel writes in *Aware*, "If we learn to dissociate from the pain of our reality, we can survive a childhood of tremendous betrayal, sadness, pain, and fear. But dissociation from pain is not selective; we inevitably disconnect even from the joy of being alive" (Siegel, 340). Like broken ceramic pots, we are perpetually drained no matter how often God pours his goodness into our hearts. The small internal cracks of fragmentation quickly deplete the faith, hope, and love the Lord offers us. Instead of experiencing an interior life full of peace and joy, we are left with an ache of loneliness and emptiness. This is why psychological self-abandonment cannot lead to wholeness or holiness. We need a whole self to abandon ourselves to God's will and fully receive what he desires for us, which includes our healing.

Reclaiming Our True Self

Many psychologists, including Dr. Charles Whitfield, believe the true self is our inner child. In *Healing the Child Within*, Whitfield writes, "The Child Within refers to that part of each of us which is ultimately alive, energetic, creative and fulfilled; it is our Real Self—who we truly are" (Whitfield, 9). Dr. Margaret Paul, in her book *Inner Bonding*, writes something similar: "The Inner Child is the aspect of our personality that is soft, vulnerable, and feelings oriented—our 'gut' instinct. It is who we are when we were born, our core self, our natural personality, with all its talent, instinct, intuition, and emotion" (Paul, 21). For who is more real than the child who has no pretense or false self? Who is more real than the child who prances around in her dress, fully invigorated in the present moment, or the child who falls to his knees and honestly tells you how upset he is?

However, as authentic as children are, they cannot represent a whole self. They are still missing something vital. Psychologist Carl Jung, who has been credited with coining the term "inner child" and providing the first process for inner child work, saw the inner child as an incomplete self. He writes, "In every adult, there lurks a child—an eternal child, something that is always becoming, is never completed, and calls for unceasing care, attention, and education. That is the part of the personality which wants to develop and become whole" (Jung 1981, 170). For Christians, we understand that the reason why this "eternal child" is always becoming and never completed is because they cannot be who they fully are without God. Our inner child may be true, but they can never be whole and reach their fullest potential without their Maker. Whitfield wrote in the introduction of *Recovery of Your Inner Child* by Dr. Lucia Capacchione, "The only way to fill our emptiness is to realize the True Self within us and experientially connect it to God. When we do that and complete our unfinished business, we are healed" (12). There will always be an emptiness that only God can fill.

Becoming like God

According to the *Catechism of the Catholic Church*, to become a complete self and connect that self to God, we must recognize that we are a child of God and share in God's divinity:

> For this is why the Word became man, and the Son of God became the Son of man: so that man, by entering into communion with the Word and thus receiving divine sonship, might become a son of God. For the Son of God became man so that we might become God. The only-begotten Son of God, wanting to make us sharers in his divinity, assumed our nature, so that he, made man, might make men gods. (CCC, 460)

It's important to note that this does not mean we become God in the polytheist sense. We do not share in God's divine nature like Jesus or the Holy Spirit—however, our true selves can share in the likeness of God.

Jesus says in John's gospel, "Holy Father, keep them in your name, which you have given me, that they may be one, even as we are one" (17:11). As we rediscover and recover our authentic selves and become more saturated in God's divine life, we begin to reflect God's image. All that we hold within us will begin to reveal not only the truth about ourselves but the truth about the love we were fashioned for.

Sharing in God's Divine Life

We may think in order to share in God's divine life and become more like him we will have to make ourselves very big. We might be tempted to make ourselves mighty and important, but as Christians, the way we share in God's divine life and become more like him is the opposite. Instead of pursuing self-righteousness, we are called to humility and littleness. God calls us to become like a child.

In Matthew's gospel, the disciples come to Jesus and ask, "Who is the greatest in the kingdom of heaven?" Jesus responds by placing a child among them and says, "Truly, I say to you, unless you turn and become like children, you will never enter the kingdom of heaven. Whoever humbles himself like this child, he is the greatest in the kingdom of heaven. Whoever receives one such child in my name receives me" (Mt 18:1, 3–5).

During Jesus's time, this was certainly a radical message. Children were often disregarded and cast aside (which isn't too far from how we treat ourselves sometimes). Jesus could have brought someone much more "important" before the disciples, but he brought a child instead. Jesus exalts what is meek, humble, and lowly and invites us to embrace and become a child, because as we do, we embrace and become like God.

Know Thy Parts, Know Thyself

From this place of embracing our most authentic self and recognizing God within this self, we can begin to explore our severance from God and our severance from our authentic core, or what I call our "imago dei." We will explore our imago dei more in the next chapter. In inner child work, we call the severances from our authentic core "parts," namely the "wounded child" (our fractured self) and the "angry child"/"adolescent self" (our protective part). These "parts" represent the sub-personalities of our inner child that have developed over time due to our imperfect nature and the imperfect nature of others. They tell the story of our pain and why we have been disconnected from living in the image and likeness of God. We also have a "Spirit-led adult self," who is our redemptive part. They are the part of us that seeks to be more saturated in faith, hope, and love and most likely responded to the invitation to read this book. We will be relying on this part a lot to help us participate in God's healing work.

Other modalities and therapists use different names, but I have found these descriptions to be most helpful and true to the wisdom of the Church, sacred scripture, and our intelligently and divinely created minds and bodies. We will explore and befriend these child parts throughout the rest of our journey together.

Reparented by God

As we venture deeper into these different "parts" of ourselves, we may find it difficult to love them. It is much easier to love those who comply, who are "easy" and well-tempered, and let people love the parts of us that seem more acceptable and polished. But this isn't typically what we find within ourselves. We typically find unruly, complicated, and emotionally immature children. Children who annoy, frustrate, and challenge our limitations. Children who ignite anger, impatience, exhaustion, and bring us to our knees in utter despair. This is why, as imperfect and limited human beings, we need a perfect and limitless family to help us heal and tend to our internal family.

Fortunately, we are given this perfect family in God. God's very nature is a community of perfect love. In the words of St. John Paul II, "God in his deepest mystery is not solitude, but a family, since he has in himself fatherhood, sonship, and the essence of family, which is love" (John Paul II 1979). God knows that we can do nothing without his perfect family of love (see John 15:5). Therefore, God relentlessly and fiercely pursues our child self and dives into the depths of our wounds and self-protections without getting crushed or confused by its heavy weight. God reaches into the complex dynamics, roles, and patterns we have developed and brings us truth. God takes what has been destroyed by the small deaths we have endured and resurrects new life. This is the power of God's family. Therefore, we can look to God as our *Abba*, or "father" in Aramaic. We can allow God to transform whatever parenting we received that prevented us from living as a secure child and growing as a mature adult. We can let God build upon our human foundation and help us become true sons and daughters.

As we allow ourselves to be received and reparented by the family of God, we will find that our false sense of self-sufficiency will be redeemed. Every part of us that has lost their way and forgotten the truth of who they really are will find their way back home. Therefore, we can surrender our control and alleviate the pressure we place on ourselves or others to reparent us completely. We can look to the parent who "comforts her child" (see Isaiah 66:13) and bring our inner child to hands that promise to gather us "as a hen gathers her brood under her wings" (Lk 13:34). We can surrender our control and trust that the Lord's instruction will give our inner child peace (See Isaiah 54:13) and a love they never knew could be possible.

Love Heals

God never wanted us to keep all the love we cultivate for ourselves. We all play a part in not only restoring our internal family but restoring our extended family—the Church and our communion with all God's children. Befriending our inner child is meant to move us from the leper, the unclean, the blind, and the Samaritan in ourselves to the leper, the unclean, the blind, and the Samaritan in others. When we can love the most vulnerable within and outside of us, we truly live and embody God's most important threefold command: "'You shall love the Lord your God with all your heart, and with all your soul, and with all your mind, and with all your strength.' The second is this, 'You shall love your neighbor as yourself'" (Mk 12:30–31).

In *Gaudium et Spes* (*Joy and Hope*), Pope Paul IV writes, "Indeed, the Lord Jesus, when He prayed to the Father, 'that all may be one . . . as we are one' (John 17:21–22) opened vistas closed to human reason, for He implied a certain likeness between the union of the divine Persons, and the unity of God's sons in truth and charity. This likeness reveals that man, who is the only creature on earth which God willed for itself, cannot fully find himself except through a sincere gift of himself" (24). Thus, as we seek to better understand and befriend our inner child, we will also better understand and befriend the inner child in others, and through that process, learn how to offer ourselves as a sincere gift. When we change our outlook on our wounds and the wounds of others and see them as a person, a little child, who is not an inconvenience or nuisance, but someone in need of love, it opens us up to love like God does and live a life of profound compassion.

Our Compassionate God

The word compassion comes from the Latin root pati, which means "to suffer," and the prefix *com*, which means "with." From this definition, *compassion* means "to suffer with." Oftentimes we think of compassion as evoking positive emotions which is often the same way we view love. We may even believe that the most compassionate and loving response to our woundedness is to remove it altogether. But God shows us that the most compassionate and loving response to our internal fracture is actually "suffering with." When God entered our fallen nature through Jesus, he drew close to our wounds and bore our pains and sorrows. Jesus could have made Judas more trustworthy, Peter more gentle, Mary Magdalene more secure, or Thomas more faithful with a snap of his finger, but he didn't. He did not eradicate what was fragile and wounded within us but approached it with compassion.

The disciples were free to question, doubt, and even betray Jesus, and Jesus still did not abandon them. Our Lord saw the child within, and through the person of Jesus, God drew closer to all that they felt and experienced, uttering, "Let the children come to me" (Lk 18:16). Let the lowly, rejected, mistrusting, insecure, fearful, and needy come to him. He extends the same invitation to us today, even when we have abandoned him or ourselves.

This allows us to follow our Lord's example and draw near to our own inner child and the inner child in others. We can "suffer with" because as we do, as we see in the suffering and death of Christ, it heals us. It brings us new life. Therefore, the work of befriending our inner child is one of the most loving actions we'll ever do. By "suffering with," we get to the heart of what we hold inside. We begin to understand ourselves and others deeply. We learn how to be empathetic and charitable. Patient and humble. Gentle and kind. We desperately need this work for ourselves and for all those whom we encounter.

For some of us, we may not be too convinced. We may be afraid of being more compassionate. We may fear that if we "suffer with," we will get stuck in the past or become too overwhelmed by the pain that we can no longer fulfill our present responsibilities. We may think, "Compassion is not productive enough," or we may recognize our limitations. Perhaps we are in a season where we are spread thin, we have very limited time or mental, emotional, or spiritual capacity and we are afraid that if we enter into the depths of compassion, we will see ourselves or others as victims. We will be entering into pity and infantilizing instead of empowering and maturing. As valid as these fears are, we must not worry about the results or our own capacity. We must trust that God will equip us and bring about a greater good because God has called us to a life of compassion. For, as St. Paul writes in his Second Letter to the Corinthians, "Blessed be the God and Father of our Lord Jesus Christ, the Father of mercies and God of all comfort, who comforts us in all our affliction, so that we may be able to comfort those who are in any affliction, with the comfort with which we ourselves are comforted by God" (1:3–4).

We also must not confuse compassion with pity. Compassion, unlike pity, moves us to act. When we are compassionate, we draw closer to the most needy within and outside of us out of love, so that together, we are heard, seen and known. And when we are heard, seen, and known, we are empowered to move forward in a way that helps us to be more present and alive. We are not stuck. We are liberated.

And as beautiful and uniting as compassion can be, it can also be burdensome, lonely, and challenging, especially if we have little experience with people showing compassion to us. So we must be patient with ourselves. It takes tremendous courage to keep practicing and choosing to be compassionate to what is lost and hurting. It also takes a considerable amount of learning, unlearning, and relearning:

- We may need to learn that compassion can be holy and healing and to unlearn pulling ourselves up by the bootstraps and ignoring our feelings and pain.

- We may need to learn that befriending our inner child is not selfish, nor does it make us a victim, and to unlearn self-abandonment, codependency, and living with a false self to survive.

- We may need to learn how to live in the family of God and be reparented by God and to unlearn seeking to get all of our needs met from those who are limited and imperfect, including our own self.

- We may need to learn how to "suffer with" with humility and prudence and to unlearn "suffering with" out of duty, obligation, or fear.

To begin this process of learning, unlearning, and even relearning, we will need to become curious. We need to start asking ourselves questions such as these: *Why am I feeling this way? What might this body ache be communicating? Why do I respond so intensely to this? I wonder what this person may really be saying to me right now. I wonder what might be triggered for this person. I wonder if this is my inner child coming out.* Questions and wonderings like these propel us forward and move us closer to our inner child and the inner child in others. They broaden our awareness and help us to begin genuinely knowing ourselves and others and, from there, truly loving ourselves and others.

So as we begin to compassionately "suffer with" and befriend our inner child, take a moment now just to pause and get curious. See if you can remember your child self. Perhaps a picture of yourself already came to mind while reading this, but try to really imagine this child again. What is your child self like? What is their body language? What are they wearing? What might your child self need? How do you see this child in your adult life?

This child, whom you saw and reflected on, is the key to healing. It is the missing piece, the long-forgotten friend, the familiar stranger, the true self that needs your compassion now and will lead you to wholeness. I cannot promise that your distressing feelings or negative thoughts will go away for good or that your harmful memories will never resurface again. I cannot promise that you will never react from a child part and destructively respond to your pain. I also cannot promise that you will never repeat a learned behavior from your family of origin or find yourself locked in a familiar dysfunctional cycle or pattern.

I can assure you, however, that throughout the rest of this book—and if you are consistent with befriending your inner child, then throughout the rest of your life—you will experience healing. You will become more Christ-like in the face of your woundedness, you will be quicker to repair, you will learn to love every part of you, and with an outpouring of love, you will also offer God the love and adoration he deserves and the compassion the world needs. You will befriend your inner child and discover new ways to share the graces you receive with another inner child in need.

Prayer

Father, thank you for my inner child. I want to befriend my inner child. I no longer want to abandon myself or allow myself to be disconnected from all that is within me. Help me remain open, curious, and attentive to the ways you are inviting me into your compassionate love so that my inner child and I can be one in you. Amen.

Befriending Work: Getting Curious

- What are the ways you have abandoned yourself? How has this harmed you and your healing?

- When you felt distress, difficult emotions, or painful experiences as a child, how did people respond to you? Are you repeating any of those behaviors now?

- Recount the ways God has reparented you. Consider what God is showing you that has been different from what you learned as a child. What might you be unlearning, learning, or relearning in your life right now?

Guided Meditation

To listen to my guided meditation for this chapter, scan the QR code below or go to https://www.avemariapress.com/befriending-inner-child-meditations.

2

Reclaiming Your Imago Dei

When I smile wide, move my body with unshaken freedom, laugh uncontrollably, extend forgiveness without reservation, look up at the night sky and experience awe, paint with my daughter, make silly faces with my son, or allow myself to be held in my husband's arms, I see my inner child who is fully alive. I see a little girl who is giddy, energetic, playful, genuine, and creative. She is full of wonder and God's light. She is a little girl who is living love.

When my clients begin this work and explore their own inner child, they usually describe a very similar child. They can identify a child within them who is unapologetically themselves. A child who is confident and self-assured and who reveals characteristics of themselves that have been long forgotten. Shy clients can sometimes see a child who is talkative and even boisterous. Clients who describe themselves as jaded or mistrusting can sometimes see a child who is soft, curious, and open to others. Clients who feel estranged from God or who are working through the felt sense of abandonment from God will often see a child run and leap into Jesus's arms with reckless abandonment. These hidden aspects of ourselves reemerge because when we create space for our inner child, our inner child unearths who we truly are—a child who has been knit together by our Creator and who is fearfully and wonderfully made (see Psalm 139:13–14). Therefore, the child within us who bears the image and likeness of God without any wounds or self-protection to darken it is our authentic core. We are the image of God, or *imago dei* in Latin.

Being the imago dei is our birthright. It is who we are meant to be. Our imago dei motivates, inspires, and fills us with hope. It is the child within who can trust, hope, play, wonder, laugh, connect with others, and delight. When connected to this inner child, our minds are filled with creativity, our bodies with peace, and our hearts with a capacity to fully receive love. We are free to be naked, seen, heard, and known fully.

As adults, we often are far removed from our inner child and our authentic core—our imago dei. We struggle to imagine this fearfully and wonderfully made child within and to experience being childlike. We have lived guided by other child parts of ourselves for so long, and there are so many people, things, and adult responsibilities that steal our attention. We have no idea how to reclaim something pure, special, and worthy of being praised within us when we are distracted, busy, and overwhelmed or when we feel wounded or stuck in survival mode.

When we can catch a glimpse of this child and experience our imago dei, however, it is like watching a shooting star spring across a night sky. The imago dei pauses us and fills us with awe and wonder, and the more we can reclaim this child, the more something physically, emotionally, and spiritually shifts within us. It is what psychologist John Bradshaw calls a "homecoming." We start to feel ourselves again. We experience something that seems natural, distant, and yet familiar.

When we experience this homecoming, we feel a calling to champion and protect this core aspect of who we are and to take responsibility for being made in the image and likeness of God. We may also find that our hearts are overcome with grief as we remember what life has been like without this vital truth of who we are. When clients complete a guided meditation to connect with their imago dei for the first time, I usually hear sentiments such as these: "I can't believe I forgot about her." "It's been so long since I have seen myself like this." "Wow, I cannot believe how precious I was . . . or maybe still am." "I miss this little child." These sentiments point to the rediscovery of our authentic self, a rediscovery typically accompanied by tears. The tears communicate what we all sense—that we have lost something sacred within ourselves. We have been disconnected from the deepest truth of who we are.

As we begin to see ourselves through this revered lens, we remember and restore the goodness of our child self. It does not matter how many painful experiences we have endured or how far we have traveled from this authentic core; without fail, our imago dei is always present, inviting us home. Our imago dei reveals that nothing can ever separate us from God in us. God created us in such a way that we are constantly connected to him, even without our conscious awareness and even when we have strayed from and abandoned our own selves.

Our imago dei communicates that we are good and worthy of love because God is good and worthy of love. Also, because his goodness and love never fail, we can trust that his goodness and love do not fail in us either. When we reconnect to this healing truth and God's expansive love for each of us, we can begin the journey of befriending our inner child. We can experience true safety and security in our minds, hearts, souls, and bodies and receive all that will bring us healing.

The Imago Dei and Our Nervous System

Our bodies will communicate to us when we experience our imago dei through our nervous system. Our nervous system is an internal surveillance system that informs us when we are safe to be who we are created to be or when our core identity is being threatened.

Our Creator has given us this surveillance system as a resource to keep us safe and connected. The more positive experiences and support we receive to champion our imago dei, the more our nervous system will regulate and keep us anchored. Our brain will work with our nervous system to input our positive experiences and make the connection that it is okay to rest and receive.

This trait within our nervous system translates to what psychologist and founder of polyvagal theory Dr. Stephen Porges identifies as the ventral vagal part of our nervous system, otherwise known as our social engagement system. When we are in our ventral vagal state, we are safe. There is no threat. We are free to express the image and likeness of God within us. We do not have to change ourselves, work hard to heal, or try to survive. Our heart rate is regulated, our breath is natural and full, and we can tune in and connect to ourselves, God, and others in mind, body, and spirit.

Think about the last time you did something that brought wonder, awe, creativity, or passion. You most likely were grounded in your ventral vagal state. You felt connected. You weren't immersed in your woundedness or trying to protect yourself. You were able to be present, and because of that, you felt whole again. God gives us these experiences to help us remember our imago dei so that we can experience wholeness not just cognitively, emotionally, or spiritually but physically in our bodies. As embodied people, we move from knowing we are created in the image and likeness of God to feeling it viscerally.

Safe and Secure

In childhood, our caregivers helped us experience the embodiment or disembodiment of our imago dei. If our caregivers were safe and provided physical and emotional security, we could claim our imago dei wholeheartedly and rest in our God-given identity. Our social engagement system was activated. We most likely saw soft eyes and loving smiles, felt tickling kisses, were held close, heard warm and loving voices, and experienced heart-to-heart contact. This level of social engagement was nothing we could understand cognitively. There was no consciousness of how this helped us live from our imago dei, but when our caregivers met these needs, we experienced living the image and likeness of God in our bodies. Our little hearts were regulated, our bodies warm, our bellies full, and we could freely express ourselves. In attachment studies, this looks like developing a secure attachment.

Attachment researcher Mary Ainsworth defines a secure attachment as trusting one's caregivers for protection and comfort (Ainsworth). Secure children can reach out when distressed and are readily calmed by a caregiver's support or their reappearance after separation. In her research on early childhood attachment, Ainsworth categorized four dimensions of a mother's behavior with her children that made the difference between a secure and insecure attachment:

- sensitivity or insensitivity

- acceptance or rejection

- cooperation or interference

- accessible or ignoring

Ainsworth's research concluded that the more sensitive, accepting, cooperative, and accessible mothers were, the more they could develop a secure attachment to their children. In contrast, anxiously attached children do not feel they can truly depend on their mothers. They are unsure whether their mother is safe and can provide the security they need, which causes them to engage in avoidant, ambivalent, or disorganized behavior during stressful times. Instead of being able to rest in the truth of their identity, they become confused, insecure, fearful, and anxious.

Therefore, when we develop a secure attachment, we develop an internal working model that tells us we are good, lovable, and whole. There is nothing fractured or missing within us or outside of us. We can internalize the security and safety our caregivers provide, which becomes part of our understanding of who we are. It does not matter if our caregivers briefly go away or miss an opportunity to connect with us; there is an assurance that their love grounds us and moves through our very being.

We all have borne witness to secure children living from their imago dei: children who ask for what they need and trust they will get their needs met, openly share their feelings, take risks, freely make mistakes, confidently express themselves, use their five senses to take in the world around them, and lean into their different feelings. When these children are happy, they dance and sing. When they are sad, they allow themselves to cry. When they are angry, they shout and fall to the floor. When tired, they allow themselves to rest. They are completely free.

It is important to note that developing a secure attachment style does not mean the child experiences perfection. No family on earth is perfect; therefore, no child is perfect. However, children who develop a secure attachment can accept their imperfect family. They can recognize they are still loved, even when experiencing imperfection, because when they experienced their own imperfection—stress, discomfort, pain, loss, resistance, fear, anger, anxiety, sadness—they were met with a consistent response of acknowledgment and attunement. They were not abandoned in their distress and human frailty.

Unfortunately, many of us did not develop a secure attachment. Many of us grew up with caregivers who were not only imperfect but living with their own abandoned inner child. These caregivers were not connected to their imago dei and therefore could not help us to remain securely connected to our own. Without this inner security and connection to our imago dei, we began to internalize our negative experiences and form our own interpretation of who we are and our purpose in this world. We also may not have been affirmed or received the truth of who we really are, which only made it easier to adopt negative beliefs about ourselves. Perhaps our caregivers prioritized tending to our physical health rather than our emotional health. Perhaps they never received affirmations and, therefore, struggled to affirm us. Perhaps they only affirmed us when we were achieving something or going above and beyond expectations.

Whatever the case, when we cannot root ourselves in our imago dei in childhood, our internalizations of the imperfection we experienced become what Dr. Aaron Beck, the founder of cognitive behavioral therapy, calls "core beliefs." Many of these core beliefs stem from an internal sense of danger. When our nervous system and brain receive information telling us we are unsafe, we internalize the unsafety and we move from our ventral vagal state to what Dr. Stephen Porges calls a sympathetic state (fight or flight) or parasympathetic dorsal vagal state (freeze).

When we can no longer rest in who we really are, we develop core beliefs that are far from confidence in being made in the image and likeness of God. Without a deep connection to our imago dei, we cannot experience a felt sense of safety and security. We are disconnected from our social engagement system, and over time our attachment becomes insecure. Instead of seeing ourselves as connected, loved, safe, and enough, we adopt beliefs such as these:

- I am all alone.

- I am unlovable.

- I am not safe.

- I am not enough or I am no good.

We will explore these core beliefs more in the next chapter.

We can even internalize perpetual feeling states. For example, if a child is constantly bored, their experience can be internalized as "I am boring," or if a child is often sad, they can internalize the core belief "I am sad," or "My life is sad." When a negative core belief is adopted, it casts a shadow on our imago dei. It becomes increasingly difficult to live in the light of who we are. Instead of living in celebration of God's goodness alive in us, we begin an exhausting search for the truth, fighting to uncover whether or not we are loved, good, worthy, and safe.

The good news is that God has given each of us an opportunity to develop earned security, no matter our attachment style. Earned security is accomplished when an adult with an insecure attachment style meets their unmet needs from childhood and adopts security. We can achieve earned security by moving from our rigid and faulty understanding of self and developing a new self-perception. We can also experience earned security when we interact with supportive adults. Our healthy adult relationships help us transform our implicit memories and our internalized narrative of the past and adopt a new and more liberating self-concept.

From this place of security, even those of us with the most dysfunctional family systems and those who have experienced even the most unspeakable traumas can develop what will help us nurture and live from our authentic core. When we redefine ourselves and see the truth of our existence, we may confidently proclaim, "We are the imago dei, God's beloved."

God's Beloved

Developing earned security and reclaiming the truth of who we truly are means that we must also reclaim that we are loved. When we are loved and receive that love well, we live out our belovedness and experience healing. This love that I am referring to is something that no human can fully offer us. It is a love that transcends our human limitations and capabilities. It is a love that communicates that no matter what we have experienced and will experience in the future, we will be carried and comforted.

In *Life of the Beloved,* Fr. Henri Nouwen magnificently captured this kind of love when he wrote:

> Our preciousness, uniqueness, and individuality are not given to us by those who meet us in clock-time— our brief chronological existence—but by the One who has chosen us with an everlasting love, a love that existed from all eternity and will last through all eternity. We may look to our parents, friends, partner, work, academics, or a stranger we meet to confirm for us that we are loved, that we matter, but these people and things can never truly offer us the affirmation and truth we desire. We can only experience this true understanding through God. (Nouwen, 49)

As God's beloved, we can hold on to this truth and not only reclaim our imago dei but live as God's child again. So often, we cannot heal because we are looking for all that is not God to love us. We want people and things to be the parent, friend, teacher, or spouse who couldn't affirm, nurture, accept, hear, see, pursue, connect, protect, or delight in us. As a result, we embark on a disappointing search that leads us deeper into our internal fragmentation. Therefore, we must remember not only who we truly are but whose we truly are. We are God's beloved, and if we want to heal, we must accept that he is the only being capable of truly healing us.

Accepting this foundational truth gives us the freedom to live as God's beloved child and partake in God's light. Jesus says in Matthew's gospel that we are the "light of the world" and that "a city set on a hill cannot be hidden" (5:14). As we learn to be the light of the world through reclaiming our imago dei, we will notice that what once used to disturb us no longer steals our peace. The darkness in our negative thoughts, distressing feelings, disturbing memories, and deepest fears is illuminated so that these no longer hold any power over us. "For you were once darkness, but now you are light in the Lord. Live as children of light" (Eph 5:8–14).

Living in the Goodness of the Imago Dei

We can begin experiencing God's light within us right away by remembering the goodness of our imago dei. We can start by remembering our unique talents, gifts, and strengths to accomplish this. We can remember what made us come alive, what felt natural and genuine, how people described us, and the positive characteristics of our child self. Sometimes our adult experiences will communicate who our imago dei is. We can recall times in adulthood when we felt energized, creative, playful, courageous, and connected. These experiences offer us a glimpse of our imago dei.

Befriending Work: Remembering Our Imago Dei

Take a moment to think about your imago dei now.

- What does this child look like? What is this child wearing? What is their hair like? What is their body language like? If you have trouble remembering, consider going through old childhood photos and videos or contacting a loved one to help you recall your imago dei. Take a moment to write these descriptions down in your journal.

- Now think about the positive characteristics you displayed in childhood or have seen throughout your life. Use the list of Imago Dei Characteristics below to help guide you. Take a moment to write your own positive characteristics down in your journal.

- Then think about your childhood hobbies, interests, and dreams. Take a moment to write these down too. What do these say about your imago dei?

List of Imago Dei Characteristics

- action-oriented
- adaptable
- adventurous
- affectionate
- analytical
- artistic
- assertive
- athletic
- bold
- brave
- calm
- caring
- cautious
- charismatic
- cheerful
- choleric
- clever
- competitive
- confident
- considerate
- courageous
- creative
- curious
- decisive
- dedicated
- detail-oriented
- determined
- down-to-earth
- dreamer
- driven
- easygoing
- efficient
- empathetic
- energetic
- entertainer
- enthusiastic
- factual
- faithful
- fast
- focused

- forgiving
- full of zest
- funny
- future-minded
- generous
- genuine
- goal-oriented
- good listener
- handy
- honest
- hopeful
- humble
- idealist
- imaginative
- influential
- innovative
- insightful
- inspiring
- integrity
- intelligent
- interdependent
- intuitive
- kind
- leader
- loves to learn
- loving
- loyal

- magnetic
- meticulous
- mindful
- observant
- open-minded
- outgoing
- passionate
- people-person
- perceptive
- persistent
- persuasive
- planner
- playful
- positive
- problem solver
- pure
- quick-witted
- reflective
- reliable
- resilient
- resourceful
- risk-taker
- self-assured
- sensitive
- socially intelligent
- spirited
- spiritual

- spontaneous
- strong faith
- strong-willed
- thinker

- thoughtful
- visionary
- warm
- wholehearted

Living Our Natural Strengths and Passions

Another way to reconnect with our imago dei is to use our strengths. Our strengths are a part of our unique light, and when we use our strengths, we give glory to God and bring integration to our child parts. The light within us shows our inner child the way out of what may feel hopeless, frustrating, or paralyzing. We become reawakened to our deeper purpose and reconnected to our imago dei, whose very essence embodies our strengths.

Our passions, interests, and hobbies are also a part of our strengths. We are drawn to them because they communicate essential truths about our goodness and God's goodness. Several of my adult clients connect with their imago dei simply by doing things they love. They rock climb, intentionally sing in the shower, play in the mud with their kids, write short stories or poetry, hike, dance, build Lego sets, complete puzzles, or watch funny movies. These are all excellent ways to reconnect with our imago dei and live as God's beloved child.

Molly's Story

Molly came to meet me because her husband was unfaithful. She did not know how she felt about it or what to do; she only knew she needed support. We started the inner child work process so that Molly could better understand who she is and develop a greater sense of how God might be calling her to respond to her situation.

When I introduced the concept of the imago dei to her, she struggled to get started. She could hardly remember her childhood and what was special or unique about herself. I then gave her a list of adjectives to see if any stood out. As she looked at the list of words, she began recalling traits she saw in herself in early childhood and adult life. I wrote them down one by one and then explored with her what she loved to do as a child, including her passions and hobbies. We also explored some of the protective factors (the needs that were met) in early childhood, and I gave her an opportunity to extend gratitude to the people who had given her gifts of connection, nurture, and love.

After we were done, I led her in a meditation where we invited Jesus and the Holy Spirit to give her an image of her imago dei. I helped her remember this child by sharing the list of her traits, passions, and hobbies she enjoyed.

As I declared this to her out loud, Molly began to sob. She had seen herself the way God sees her for the first time. I prompted her to introduce herself to her imago dei and even apologize for forgetting her. Molly could see her imago dei, so full of forgiveness and faith, responding to her apology by quickly shrugging her shoulders and, with childlike innocence, uttering, "It's okay." Then she saw her imago dei climbing on Jesus's lap with complete trust. She could see how delighted he was to see her child self. He seemed so proud of her—something she had never experienced before. Instead of feeling shame and rejection, feelings she knew too well, in Jesus's presence, all she could feel was abounding love. We ended the meditation with her entrusting this little girl to Jesus and saying her goodbyes for now.

When we processed what she experienced, she could feel peace radiating in her body. Something had physically lifted in her body—she was in her ventral vagal state (connection, safety, rest), and because of that, she could feel unburdened. She had been the responsible and dutiful wife and mother for so long that she forgot that there was a child within her who was good and special. She forgot how much Jesus delighted in her and that it could be safe to rest in her belovedness.

Now Molly uses her strengths to tenderly draw near to other child parts, just as she was able to do with her imago dei. Molly lives with much more freedom, self-compassion, and self-awareness. She knows what she feels, including where she feels those feelings in her body, what she desires and needs, and how to express that effectively to others. She has learned to integrate the little girl she experienced in the meditation and trust Jesus from her core. This interior freedom enables her to love her husband with a kind of love that wouldn't make sense to many people and to delight in the world around her, even in the unknown. Molly has also started dreaming again. She felt inspired to explore a new career and become more involved in the Church, something she did not allow herself to do in the past out of fear of failure and disappointing others.

I have never seen a picture of Molly's child self, but I must tell you that when she started connecting with her imago dei, I started to see her. A brilliant light radiates within her. Whenever I meet with Molly, she smiles and laughs in the face of adversity and carries a quiet fearlessness. I cannot help but smile and feel my body resting in my ventral vagal state in her presence.

Molly's is one of many stories where the imago dei awakens us to live our most authentic selves. We cannot begin befriending our inner child without recognizing this child within who bears the image and likeness of God. For it is this child who belongs in God's kingdom (see Luke 18:16), and it is this child who will lead us to wholeness and healing.

Prayer

Father, I am starting to see my imago dei. I am starting to see and reclaim how wonderful you made me and how I bear your image and likeness. Help me to live from my authentic core and experience this child within me again. Amen.

Befriending Work: Exploring Your Imago Dei Further

- When do you encounter your imago dei in your adult life? What do you typically feel (emotionally and somatically) in these encounters? What has made you disconnect from your imago dei?

- If you found a photograph of yourself from early childhood that best captures the essence of your imago dei, spend several moments just delighting in the image. Notice how you feel when you look at this image. Now place the image in a place where you can see it regularly. When you look at it, practice thinking a loving thought about yourself.

- Choose one of the hobbies, activities, or interests that makes your imago dei come alive, and make time to do it this week. Notice how you feel as you do this activity, and if it brings up anything for you, write it in your journal.

Guided Meditation

To listen to my guided meditation for this chapter, scan the QR code below or go to https://www.avemariapress.com/befriending-inner-child-meditations.

3

Nurturing Your Wounded Child

I wish we could always feel the presence of our imago dei. We all long to live with peace, joy, hope, playfulness, zeal, connection, and presence. Yet, on this side of heaven, we must accept that it is not always possible. In fact, from a nervous system perspective, it is impossible to stay always in our ventral vagal state and experience our social engagement system. Many demands, fears, and triggers take us from the experience of our authentic core to different nervous system states that move us into a stress response. Although it may be disappointing and lead to many distressing feelings, it is a healthy testament to our body doing what it needs to do to maintain integration. However, what is unhealthy is becoming disconnected from our ventral vagal state for a long period of time.

When we are wounded, our sympathetic nervous system (fight or flight), dorsal vagal state (freeze) or a combination of both (fawn), becomes activated. Our body moves from the place of resting in our belovedness to fighting for our survival. Being stuck in survival states creates a subpersonality or part. We become fragmented, with a new self-concept, core beliefs, and core feelings vastly different from our being made in the image and likeness of God.

Trauma studies have identified this fragmentation as "structured dissociation" or "childhood trauma splitting." When we experience childhood trauma, we disconnect from our imago dei to survive. This is not something we do consciously, but it is a natural occurrence when we are trying to manage our distress in childhood. As children, we simply do not have the skills and resources, nor have built enough tolerance, to be able to stay rooted in who we are when we experience threats to our very existence. Even if we have not experienced childhood trauma, perhaps we did not experience our imago dei being championed and nurtured. We did not experience praise for our unique characteristics, gifts, talents, or emotional attunement, or responsiveness to our needs. As a result, we struggled to feel delighted in, really understood, and appreciated for who we truly are.

In many ways, we are all "wounded children" because of our original sin. St. Thomas Aquinas taught that although we are made in the image and likeness of God, we are not free from concupiscence. In our fallen nature, we will always bear the mark of original sin and the inclination to choose sin in this life. Although we are created in the image and *likeness* of God, we can never mirror God completely. We see this fracture in small children. We can recognize their imago dei poignantly and yet also recognize something within them that wants to test the limits, push back, question authority, and cling to what feels pleasurable.

Brain studies show that many of these behaviors result from an unformed and disintegrated brain. Our prefrontal cortex (the rational part of our brain) does not fully develop until twenty-five years old, and yet we can still see this propensity to be self-absorbed, impatient, and rebellious way beyond twenty-five. Therefore, our inner child bears the mark of our fallen nature and the image of our immaturity—what still must develop within us. However, this does not detract from our inner child's value. God still loves us. We are chosen and adopted as God's children, and because of that, God will give us the grace to reclaim wholeness, even in our woundedness and immaturity.

Our greatest blessing is what God offers us through Jesus's death and Resurrection. When Jesus died on the Cross and was resurrected in full glory, he offered us a way to live no longer fractured. He took our freedom to choose and gave us a reason to choose wholeness. He offered us hope and the promise of a fully integrated and healed self through him. God redeemed our fallen nature, but the wounded child has difficulty accessing this grace and receiving Christ's healing power. The wounded child is bound and chained to the hurts of our past and has not experienced the Lord's redemption.

To explain this further, imagine your imago dei standing before you proudly. See that child within so full of faith, hope, and love. That imago dei bears the image and *likeness* of God, but they are not God. The imago dei is always limited and imperfect, yet also undivided. This child may disobey, throw a tantrum, demand a snack, or refuse to put on clothes, but they have not lost their imago dei. The truth of their belovedness remains intact.

Then, imagine that same little child is unheard, unseen, unsafe, or unloved. They have repeated experiences of being alone. Or perhaps they are never praised unless they do something extraordinary, or they are severely punished for developmentally appropriate behavior. Or they are pushed to be and do what feels inauthentic. Or they hear messages like, "You are never going to amount to anything," "Just go away!" "I can't deal with how emotional you are being!" "Stop talking so much!" "Stop asking questions!" "I can't spend time with you—go help your siblings!" Now imagine that same beautiful child begins to hide. You can no longer see the child. All you see is this new child suddenly appearing. A child who doesn't appear so confident. A child who seems confused, lonely, and rejected. This is the wounded child.

Experiencing Our Woundedness

In a world full of disappointment, stress, pressure, and painful news, there is no avoiding the experience of our wounded child in our adult lives. Our current stressors, challenges, and sorrows will often activate this part of ourselves.

We might also sense our wounded child come up when we are all alone at night, tired, hungry, sick, overwhelmed with many tasks and responsibilities, or when we feel weak and powerless in a relationship or within a situation. We may also notice our wounded child when we become tearful and just want to cry. Or we find ourselves shy and withdrawn. We may want to go into a secret hiding place and stay there forever.

Our wounded child will often trigger these kinds of responses because the wounded child reveals our hidden negative core beliefs, unprocessed traumatic memories, the dysfunctional roles we played in our family system, and wounds. Their feelings and desires to be seen, heard, and cared for confirm that they have not been given something that is their birthright. They have been deprived of a great good God intended for us to experience. The wounded child knows this instinctively because we can only ache for something when we understand at some level that it exists. Therefore, when these instinctual needs have not been met, our wounded child may feel perpetually sad, worried, lonely, rejected, ashamed, anxious, fearful, or inadequate. We can also notice these feelings in our bodies. We might experience persistent headaches, stomachaches, tension in our shoulders, hands, and feet, or pressure in our chest or head. When we notice these feelings and unmet needs or longings, we can nurture this vulnerable part of ourselves and allow this part to experience what they need most.

Many of us have not learned how to take a closer look at our experiences and acknowledge how they affected us—those experiences that took us from our inner knowing that we have been made in the image and likeness of God. Instead, we have been primed to doubt ourselves—to "keep calm and carry our cross" and never look back. We also can be skilled at "shoulding" ourselves. Well, we *should* feel happy. We *should* feel grateful. We *should* feel peaceful, and so on. As a result, we never venture into the truth of how we actually feel.

It does not matter if we have received many blessings, live a very comfortable life, and are even feeling relatively well; the wounded child will call out for us, bulldoze past all of our "shoulds," and some way, somehow, invite us to take a closer look at our story and the experiences that are embedded in it. Therefore, we need this wounded child just as much as we need our imago dei because this child part will reveal what we need to heal and the unmet needs that will restore our wholeness.

The Fragmenting Four and the Wounded Child

Taking a closer look at the wounded child's experiences that cause fragmentation will help us move from disintegration and what I call the "fragmenting four" experiences: sin, trauma, attachment injuries, and complicated grief. In a fallen world, the fragmenting four often go hand in hand and will intersect throughout our lives, such as in the following ways:

- When we experience an attachment injury, it is often traumatic and can lead to sinful behavior.

- When we experience trauma, our attachment is severed, and it can be challenging to feel safe and secure with others and even with God. Trauma can also result from someone's sin and lead to sinful behavior.

- When we sin or experience someone else's sin, it can be traumatic or traumatize others and impact our attachment with others.

- When we experience complicated grief, it can be traumatic and negatively shape our attachment; it may be due to a person's sinful behavior, or in the absence of the person we long for, we can be led to sin.

Sin

According to the *Catechism of the Catholic Church*, sin is defined as "an offense against reason, truth and right conscience; it is a failure in genuine love for God and neighbor caused by perverse attachment to certain goods. It wounds the nature of man and injures human solidarity" (1849). For those who hold a tremendous amount of inadequacy and who have lived guided by their wounded child for a long period of time, the topic of sin can feel incredibly uncomfortable. We may start to feel shame or a desire to quickly skim past this section. But the same God who draws near to our wounds with compassion also draws near to our sin with compassion. Therefore, we can give ourselves permission to draw closer to our sin with compassion too. This does not by any means excuse our sinful behavior or the sinful behavior in others. Rather, acknowledging our sin and being compassionate towards ourselves helps us to experience true humility and accept that we all have fallen short of the glory of God.

In early childhood, sin doesn't necessarily fragment us from our imago dei, does not steal our identity, as long as it is met with humility and mercy. For example, we may have chosen to lie to our caregiver or steal a cookie when nobody was looking even after we were told not to, but if a caregiver helped us to understand right from wrong and extended Christ's forgiveness, we most likely remained rooted in our imago dei. However, if a caregiver responded harshly, humiliated us, or reprimanded us in a way that spiraled us into fear and shame, we most likely started to experience our wounded child. This is important to emphasize. God conquered sin in our lives through the love and mercy of Jesus Christ. However, if that love and mercy is not shared with us during critical moments of development when we have fallen short, then it becomes much easier not to extend love and mercy towards ourselves.

The same is true for the people who have wounded us by their sin. For example, we may have had a prideful caregiver who turned to drunkenness to protect their wounded child from further shame. They may have relied heavily on alcohol and other addictive escapes to curb their painful emotions. As a result, they may have struggled tempering their own impulses. They may have been abusive, easily angered, and vengeful or have been quick to withdrawal and retreat. They may have exploited your strength of kindness and relied on you to care for them in their addiction. When we are exposed to the sins of others and there is no humble repair and reconciliation, it can wound us deeply and distort our relationships, including how we view and relate to our own selves.

The more sin continues, it becomes easy to turn away from God and our true selves. Our imago dei becomes blurry or seemingly nonexistent. We are not able to participate in God's divine family, and thus we lose the unity within our own selves, with God, and with others.

Trauma

When we look closely at our stories and experiences, we will see that we have all experienced trauma to some degree. Even those who believe they have never experienced something traumatic can usually identify events or occasions that deserve a closer look. We must understand that trauma is not always some terrible event in our life. We cannot always see or understand it by pinpointing a distressing experience. Many trauma researchers have found that when we experience trauma, it is our body's way of managing painful and distressing experiences. Therefore, trauma can be anything that moved us out of our ventral vagal state where our imago dei lives and kept us stuck in a survival state because the experience was threatening our authentic core.

When we view trauma through this lens, we can see how it can be a beautiful gift from our Creator. Our bodies are brilliantly designed to protect our belovedness. However, the problem with trauma is that it does not know how to reestablish safety and security when the threat has been removed, and there are still minor threats or stressors that trigger the same stressful feelings. In this traumatized state, our nervous system and brain will spring into action and keep us locked in self-protection instead of self-compassion and love.

Sometimes, we may not feel very wounded by an experience. For example, many people minimize their childhood experiences with mean kids or teachers from school, an uncle or aunt who often made them feel uncomfortable, a difficult-to-please mother, or a father who was often working and had no time for connection. However, if the body responded in a way that kept us hypervigilant, walking on eggshells, hiding, people-pleasing, frozen, despondent, or always ready to fight, and there was no one there to support us, offer us safety, and help us make sense of our experience, our body stored it as a trauma. It knew this was too distressing and offered us a way to survive.

Past trauma—such as physical, sexual, or emotional abuse, harassment, bullying, neglect, being a counselor for your parent's marital problems, moving around a lot, being exposed to pornographic images at a young age, experiencing economic hardship, or being compared to a more academic, athletic, or esteemed sibling—can keep us locked in a state of survival. It hijacks higher levels of functioning. Our cognitions, rational thought processes, and ability to reason turn offline, keeping us disconnected from the truth of who we are, which is why simply telling our own wounded child truths does not typically work. For example, we can tell our wounded child, "God loves you" or "I love you," but we may still feel broken and unloved. Or someone can tell you, "It wasn't your fault. You were a little boy. There was nothing you could have done." Yet, you still go to bed thinking, "No, it was my fault. I am the problem."

We experience trauma more in childhood because children are so vulnerable. *Vulnerability* comes from a Latin word meaning "to wound." Unfortunately, our imago dei's vulnerability, the pure child within, can become easily exploited, manipulated, coerced, minimized, bypassed, and fall victim to those who hold more power. Children can also experience trauma more easily since they depend completely on their caregivers. A child's underdeveloped nervous system relies heavily on a caring adult for coregulation. A child also relies heavily on their caregiver to know who they are based on their caregiver's responses to them in their joy, sickness, longing, and pain. Since children do not have an integrated and fully formed brain, they struggle to make sense of their experiences and they are unable to inform their body that they are safe, secure, and loved. As a result, they may start to feel very unsafe, insecure, and unloved.

When a child cannot make sense of their painful, distressing, and confusing experiences, they begin to see themselves through their interpretation of their trauma. As a result, the child is no longer authentic but dissociated, as we see with childhood trauma splitting or structured dissociation. In *Adult Children of Emotionally Immature Parents*, psychologist Lindsay Gibson writes, "Children stay in alignment with their true self if the important adults in their lives support doing so. However, when they're criticized or shamed, they learn to feel embarrassed by their true desires. By pretending to be what their parents want, children think they've found a way to win their parents' love. They silence their true selves and instead follow the guidance of their role selves and fantasies. In the process, they lose touch with both their inner and outer reality" (124). When this happens, children simply exist without any felt sense of existence, realness, or identity. They are cut off from their imago dei.

We may experience our wounded child's disconnection from our imago dei when we are dissociated in adulthood—when we feel "zoned out," distracted, and disconnected from the world around us. We may find ourselves often daydreaming, scrolling, overly thinking about the past or future, or not recalling childhood experiences, let alone what happened a week ago.

If we experience derealization, it may seem that nothing feels real anymore—joy and vibrancy are sucked out of life by our own disconnection from ourselves. Thus, depersonalization becomes an even greater reality. We might start to feel as if maybe we are not real. Instead of being able to live present and embodied, it is as if we are a character in a movie.

These more extreme forms of disconnection from our imago dei help us see that when we become severed from our authentic core and live with our wounded child self running the show for too long, we are in danger of losing our imago dei and thus our true selves.

Attachment Injuries, Developmental Trauma

Another way we can lose our true selves and live led by the wounded child is through attachment injuries and developmental trauma. Attachment injuries can occur at any point, but we are more vulnerable to them during the first three years of our life. Attachment researchers define an attachment injury as anything that disrupts the bond between a caregiver and their child. Sometimes our caregivers go through illnesses, postpartum challenges, a divorce, substance abuse, domestic violence, financial insecurity, home displacement, or their own trauma that can impact their ability to bond with their children.

Attachment injuries are often traumatic and lead to developmental trauma because they threaten the core of who we are and take us from being securely rooted in our imago dei to a perpetual experience of insecurity and lack of safety. As painful as attachment injuries are, what hurts the most is typically not about what happened but what did not happen to impact our attachment. For example, we may have had an experience when our caregiver responded critically, but what hurt the most was that the same caregiver who responded critically also never affirmed us. When a caregiver does not affirm a child simply for being their authentic self or make space for their interests, strengths, feelings, needs, and desires, the caregiver rejects the child's imago dei. When a child's imago dei is rejected, that child is also abandoned. They lose the person who is supposed to keep them safe and remind them of their God-given goodness, and as a result, instead of living their belovedness, they live full of shame.

Psychologist John Bradshaw states, "Shame is internalized when the child is abandoned," and "Abandonment is the precise term to describe how one loses one's authentic self and ceases to exist psychologically" (Bradshaw, 31). Unfortunately, a child's developmentally appropriate egocentrism and vulnerability make them easy targets to internalize shame. They are prone to accepting blame and believing, "It was my fault." "I am the bad one." "It is my responsibility."

From a nervous system perspective, the wounded child often lives in a dorsal vagal state. The shame immobilizes the child, and they essentially go into a freeze response. A sense of lethargy, hopelessness, lack of agency, and powerlessness takes over gradually when they are alone with their shame and the wounds, feelings, and interlocking core beliefs.

We can also experience attachment trauma or injuries in adulthood. When we experience trauma in an intimate relationship, our bond with our partner, spouse, or best friend can be ruptured. When the person we are in an adult and intimate relationship with violates our expectation that they will offer comfort and care during our time of need, we are severely wounded. Experiences such as spousal abuse—emotional or physical abuse, neglect, sudden abandonment, or betrayals like adultery—can send us into a deeper estrangement from our imago dei.

Adult attachment injuries and trauma often echo or magnify our childhood attachment injuries, thus creating more fracture and disconnection from our imago dei. Reconsider Molly's story from the previous chapter. Molly had experienced an attachment injury from her parents. Her mother and father left Mexico to start a life in the United States during her early childhood, and she was sent to live with her grandparents. When she was reunited with her mother around age four, her mother did not know how to connect with her, and neither did Molly know how to connect with her mom.

When Molly's husband left her, this was severe attachment trauma. The person who made a vow and commitment to cherish her all the days of his life no longer wanted to stay married to her. As devastating as this was, Molly had been carrying a similar wound her whole life. Abandonment was nothing new to her, yet experiencing it again as an adult became soul-crushing.

Complicated Grief

We all know what it feels like to be abandoned to some degree, to be separated from someone we love, or to lose someone. As we see with Molly, she knew these feelings well too. But experiencing loss and the grief that comes with it does not have to fragment us. In fact, if we are well supported and have space to feel our emotions, our grief can lead us closer to love and is a necessary ingredient to healing and becoming whole.

Oftentimes, though, during our formative and primary years, our grief shakes us to our core. We are not well supported and do not have the space to feel our emotions, let alone the knowledge to name them. As a result, our loss threatens our safety and security. We begin to experience trauma symptoms (withdrawal, hopelessness, numbness, dissociation, anxiety, etc.) and can no longer experience the faith, hope, and love embedded in our authentic core. Instead, we experience a hollow emptiness and a pervasive yearning for what we have lost.

Pria's Story

Pria, a graduate student studying counseling psychology, had come to see me to work through her complicated grief. She suddenly lost her mother in a car accident when she was six. Unfortunately, it was not handled well. Her father, feeling traumatized himself, decided it was best not to tell her right away, and as a result, she learned from a family member a couple of days later. Terrified, alone, and confused, Pria had no idea what to do except shut down. She became quieter, withdrawn, and immersed herself in her schoolwork. Over the years, Pria's father rarely talked to her about the loss or asked her how she was feeling, which contributed to Pria feeling more lost and disconnected. When Pria and I started to process this, it became clear that her loss was internalized. She began to take responsibility for her mother's death and her father's response, or lack thereof. Instead of seeing her imago dei, she saw a shell of a person.

We had to do a lot of work around helping Pria imagine a life where she did not have to see things through her wounded child's lens while also allowing her wounded child to grieve appropriately. Most of our time together has been spent helping the wounded child put words to her experience, lament, cry, yearn for her mother, and be nurtured in her yearning. For so much of Pria's life, she had tried to distract herself from her wounded child and cover up her feelings through school and helping others, including her father.

Now Pria still experiences grief, which I suspect will never go away, but it is not complicated. Pria is a whole self. She can see who she truly is and live from that truth. She also is free to feel her emotions, respond to those emotions, and live a more integrated and authentic life. If our wounded child holds complicated grief, attachment injuries, trauma, or sin and has not experienced forgiveness, repentance, or mercy, our goal is to help them to experience this freedom, integration, and authenticity that Pria now lives with too. What we have suffered does not have to fragment us any longer. Our God who exists outside of time and space meets us in our brokenness and the past experiences that have invaded our present. In God's healing embrace, he gives us the opportunity to offer our wounded child what they always needed, and over time, our befriending of this child will open us up to a life that no longer feels wounding but healing.

The Generations That Came Before

When exploring our wounded child, it can also be helpful to explore our mother's experience being pregnant with us. Psychiatrist Thomas Verny writes extensively about his research into this phenomenon in his book *The Secret Life of the Unborn Child*. Verny's work emphasizes how life inside our mother's womb matters. What we experience in utero forms us as infants, and it shapes our wounded child. Many clinical studies have also shown the link between a mother's and her baby's health. The results indicate that unprocessed trauma, high stress, anxiety, depression, and grief that a mother experiences can transmit to the baby. Even though it would make sense that a baby would be living from their imago dei, these experiences can live in their bodies and disconnect them from experiencing their authentic core before they are even born.

Early in my career, I worked at a foster care agency where I was often exposed to the fragmenting four and this painful truth of transmission. Infants and small children there could not rest in their belovedness. I witnessed babies who could not be consoled, three-year-olds who wanted to die, and five-year-olds who would resist love and nurture, no matter how lovingly it was presented. These children often had caring adults in their lives, but the transmitted wounds, the stressful experiences in utero, and the trauma, attachment injuries, sin, and complicated grief they were exposed to in their early life had prevented them from experiencing their imago dei. They were immersed all too early in their wounded child part.

It also true that we not only carry our experience in the womb and our mother's own unprocessed and unhealed wounds, but our father's wounds, and the generations that came before our mother and father. In the book of Numbers, we read that our parents' sins, iniquities, and their negative consequences can affect children up to the third and fourth generations (see Numbers 14:18). Trauma research confirms this and continues to explore how our ancestors' experiences can create wounds that we carry within ourselves from the cradle to the grave.

However, if our ancestors could have transformed their traumatic experiences, broken sinful patterns, developed a secure attachment, and healed their wounded child, they most likely would not have transmitted this trauma to our wounded child. That is why it is so important to carefully examine the wounded child in ourselves and make space for their unmet needs and desires, because whether we like it or not, this part is here to stay and will live to tell a painful story long after we are gone in those who will come after us if we do not address it in ourselves.

Therefore, we must accept that the work to support this part of us will be long and arduous. Our wounded child has a permanent residency in our hearts. No matter how many times we do not want to feel their cries for protection, longings for love, or yearning for safety and security, our wounded child will continue to be the bedrock of our adult conflicts and distress until they get their needs met and have learned that they are free to rest with the imago dei.

We can begin meeting our wounded child's needs by first learning how to nurture this vulnerable part of ourselves. We will develop many nurturing skills throughout this book. As we discover and apply what we learn, we can begin ushering our wounded child back to wholeness. We can help our wounded child remember they are beloved, and through this remembering and reclaiming, they can become untethered from the wounds that have distorted their vision and kept them in darkness for so long.

To begin this untethering, let's identify what specific wounds, core beliefs, and core feelings this part of us holds.

Befriending Work: Identifying Core Wounds, Core Beliefs, and Core Feelings

Take a moment to reflect on what core wounds, negative core beliefs, and distressing feelings your wounded child might be carrying, and see if you can come up with an image that best represents this vulnerable part of yourself in your mind.

Core Wounds

- Abandonment wound: I was abandoned by someone I entrusted to care for me.

- Betrayal wound: I trusted someone I really cared about, and they betrayed me and/or our family.

- Bypassed wound: I often felt like my emotions were bypassed. They were not taken seriously.

- Complex grief wound: A caregiver or someone really close to me passed away or left me all too soon. My parents got a divorce, I lost a pet, or I moved around a lot and lost a lot of relationships and stability along the way, and I did not have anyone to support me with the emotions that came with the loss.

- Confusion wound: I was treated in a way that gave mixed signals. I experienced unpredictability often. I often felt blindsided or unsure because there was a lack of stability and communication in my home.

- Domination wound: I was often controlled. I did not get to develop my own sense of self, make choices, explore interests, or assert my own boundaries, thoughts, feelings, and opinions.

- Enmeshment wound: I was used to meeting the needs and feelings of my caregiver(s). I could not have a separate and distinct self. I often felt smothered. I had to adopt a role that pleased others and mirrored my caregiver's thoughts, feelings, interests, and needs.

- Exploitation/parentification wound: My strengths were used to the advantage of others. I did not have the freedom to be a child. I often had to take on adult responsibilities that left me feeling exploited.

- Harm wound: I was physically, psychologically, or emotionally harmed. I was yelled at, often hit, threatened, manipulated, punished harshly, or exposed to violence.

- Instability wound: I often moved around a lot. I hardly experienced any stability in my life. It was difficult to make and keep friends. I did not feel like I was ever enough.

- Judgment wound: I was judged and criticized frequently. I was publicly or privately ridiculed. I was not allowed to fail. I did not feel like I was ever enough.

- Mother or father attachment wound: I did not experience a healthy relationship with my mother or father. I did not get my attachment needs met.

- Rejection wound: When I reached out for connection, I was dismissed. I hardly felt seen, heard, or known. Many negative statements were said to me. My caregivers, siblings, or peers did not make time for me or emotionally or physically connect with me.

- Separation wound: I was separated from a caregiver. My "world" was taken away from me from an early age.

- Shame/guilt wound: I was often made to feel guilty for things that were age-appropriate or normal. I was ridiculed, rejected, harshly disciplined, or stonewalled when I made a mistake.

- Spiritual wound: I trusted a religious institution and/or person and was met with a violation of boundaries, harsh condemnation, judgment, or teaching that confused, shamed, or terrified me.

- Systemic wound: I was hurt by the education system, government, or another cultural system or community I was a part of. The system did not allow me to understand myself better or primed me to assimilate and disconnect from myself.

- Unaffirmed wound: I often did not receive praise or affirmation. I only received praise or affirmation if I accomplished something grandiose, acted perfectly, and / or acted like my caregivers.

- Unchosen wound: I often did not feel picked or chosen. I felt like I was the last option.

- Unprotected wound: Nobody was there to support me when I needed someone to protect me, stand up for me, or shelter me from harm.

- Violation wound: I could not have my own boundaries. I was intruded on and could not have my own privacy. I was emotionally, sexually, or physically violated. I was exposed to something that was not age-appropriate. I often felt as if I had no rights to my own body or belongings.

Negative Core Beliefs

- I am not worth pursuing or staying for. I am unwanted.

- I am not safe. The world is not safe.

- I have no right to my own feelings, thoughts, or body. My feelings, thoughts, or body are not safe.

- I cannot trust my own intuition.

- I am powerless.

- I do not matter. I am worthless.

- I am not ____ enough. (beautiful, special, smart, good, etc.)

- I am a reject. Nobody really cares about me. I do not belong.

- I am not worth protecting.

- I am unchosen.

- I do not belong.
- I am a fraud.
- I am bad.
- I am all alone.
- I am boring.
- I am unsafe.
- I am an unhappy person.
- I am weak.
- I am too shy.
- I am too loud.
- I am my emotions (sad, angry, anxious).
- I am attention-seeking.

Distressing Feelings

- afraid
- anxious
- ashamed
- confused
- disconnected
- empty
- helpless
- hopeless
- inadequate
- insecure
- lonely
- misunderstood
- on edge
- powerless
- rejected
- sad
- smothered
- suffocated
- unheard
- unseen
- violated
- worthless

Identifying our wounded child's core wounds, negative core beliefs, and distressing feelings is difficult. You may find your body shifting and holding pain or discomfort as you acknowledge your wounded child. You may also experience your angry child or adolescent self coming up to protect you, which can look like resistance to move forward, negative thoughts, frustration, irritation, or anger. You may even want to direct your anger to those who could not offer you what you needed—anger at the generations before you, anger at your parents, or even anger at yourself. This part of you that may be coming up is valid and integral to your healing and wholeness. In the next chapter, we will spend a lot of time understanding this part, but for now, it is important to remember that healing work is never about condemnation and blame. We must guard ourselves against pride, self-righteousness, and the beckoning for retribution.

Every person has a wounded child part, and most of us have not nurtured this part of ourselves. We weren't given the tools. We may have also given up on this part or been too afraid to venture closer. We may have even been convinced by the enemy that "this is just the way I am," but what I hope you discover is that this could not be further from the truth.

Perhaps those who have played a role in our woundedness may have been unable to heal and reclaim wholeness, but we can. We can take responsibility for how we choose to show up for our wounded child, see the truth of our imago dei, and extend Christ's mercy and compassion to ourselves and to those who wounded us. In the meantime, let us continue to take full, deep breaths and remember we are God's beloved, and that every part of us deserves to know this truth and experience it fully.

Prayer

Father, I am starting to see my wounded child. It is painful to acknowledge the ways I have been wounded and how those wounds impacted me, but I trust that you have brought me to this fractured part of myself for a reason. Help me to draw closer and befriend this part of myself, even when it is scary and painful. Amen.

Befriending Work: Exploring Your Wounded Child Further

- Seeing how much your wounded child carries, how does this make you feel? What do you notice in your body? Does this feel similar to how you felt as a child or anything you felt recently?

- When do you experience your wounded child part in adulthood? What triggers your wounded child to come out?

- What are your wounded child's unmet needs? Take a moment to pray and ask God to reveal what this part of you needs most.

- Write a letter to your wounded child and share what you want or hope for them to believe about themselves, including the needs you hope will be met.

Guided Meditation

To listen to my guided meditation for this chapter, scan the QR code below or go to https://www.avemariapress.com/befriending-inner-child-meditations.

4

Maturing Your Angry Adolescent Self

"I can't do this!" yelled Jeremiah. Jeremiah is a thirty-year-old client who struggled to connect with his wounded child during our guided meditation.

"I am just agitated, and I keep drawing a blank," Jeremiah continued.

"It's okay. Why don't we stop here and just breathe together?" I suggested.

He smirked. "Okay, I guess. Whatever you say. I am just not doing this meditation."

I tried to mirror his frustration and pull in closer to meet him. I then validated the anger. "This process can be agitating. It is okay to be a little frustrated with me or this part of our work together."

His furrowed eyebrows began to soften, and he looked at me with a slight gleam of openness in his eyes. "Yeah, it's not you. I think I am just scared to go there. I am scared I am not ready."

Jeremiah was experiencing the resistance of his angry child or adolescent self. This part did exactly what they had always done throughout his life—protect the wounded child. As we got closer to Jeremiah's most vulnerable feelings in the meditation, this part shielded his wounded child from perceived harm. The angry child or adolescent self kept him apprehensive and agitated. This part tried to convince him that this next step in our work together wasn't necessary.

Like Jeremiah, we all have a defensive part of us that wants to shield us from perceived harm. This part of us cautions, protests, or resists anything that may potentially wound us further. We can feel this part in our bodies when hotness floods toward our face or a heavy resistance pulsates through our bodies. We may feel a paralyzing tightness in our chest or fidgety restlessness in our hands, feet, and legs.

These feelings exist because the angry child or adolescent self is governed by survival. They are constantly in fight, flight, freeze, or fawn mode or, in the language of the nervous system, a sympathetic state, a dorsal vagal state, or a combination of both, and our body will reflect that.

We call this part the angry child or adolescent self because this part of us holds our anger and typically forms more rapidly in adolescence. We will explore this part's anger later and, from here on out, refer to this part as the "protective part" for brevity.

Developmentally, adolescence is when we can start to name the injustices we have experienced for the first time, including those happening in our communities and greater world, and assert our opinions, thoughts, and feelings. During this development period, we typically have more agency and will want to use our agency to right wrongs. As our brains rapidly develop and we have more language and understanding of what is happening within and around us, we will begin questioning and pushing back against what we may have previously unknowingly accepted.

Building confidence, asking questions, asserting ourselves, and understanding ourselves and the world around us are gifts. We need this period of development to grow into mature adults. However, this part of ourselves is suspended in time and cannot mature properly on their own because, despite their quick initiative and defense, they are still a child.

Longing for Justice and Healing

We can think of this part of ourselves like a scab. It is a stiff, rigid, and difficult-to-penetrate wall that forms to cover our hurt. On the surface, the protective part looks like it is doing its job, and in some ways it is, but when we remove the scab, the wound is still there. The scab cannot heal the wound fully.

Our protective part does not understand that they are not healing our wounded child's wounds. Since they are covering up the damage, they will often maintain their impenetrable shield without recognition that their defense mechanisms are also "protecting" our wounded child from love, connection, security, internal safety, trust, and peace.

Our protective part is also a restless part of ourselves. We see this restlessness in our anxiety, overthinking, busyness, and planning, as well as in our bodily tension and discomfort. Essentially, this part does not know how to surrender or has not experienced that it can be safe to surrender. Surrendering can feel threatening to our very survival. Our protective part essentially tells us, "If I lower the wall, if I surrender all the defense mechanisms I have adopted to keep you safe, we won't be okay."

We are not wrong or bad for our inner restlessness and striving to be okay. Our restlessness and striving are natural and point to the justice and healing we have been created for. Like the wounded child, our protective part cannot long and ache for something unless that something exists. We are created for something and someone who can bring us rest—something and someone who will make wrongs right, protect us, and repair our fragmentation.

However, this part does not realize that healing and justice do not come from their doing alone. The protective part can only rely on their childlike emotions, raw reactions, fantasies, idolizations, and fears to "make things right." Therefore, in an attempt to heal and bring justice, the protective part ends up wreaking havoc on our lives. Often, the sin that causes us to scurry toward Reconciliation is rooted in our protective part's self-reliance, pride, and the shame we feel toward this part of ourselves. Ultimately, our protective part does not want to sin or bring more pain to our lives, but in their desperation to alleviate our wounded child's suffering by any means necessary, they often lead us to vice and further wounding.

Without the leadership of a healthy and mature Spirit-led adult self, our protective part will often "protect" us in our adult life by helping us to

- escape or avoid difficulty;
- become overly independent or assert independence through rebellion;
- become codependent/people-pleasing or fawn;
- distract or numb ourselves from painful emotions;
- bypass our emotions (including spiritual bypassing);
- strive for a distorted view of perfection;
- smile and pretend like we have it all together;
- make everyone laugh;
- act like a "know-it-all";
- obsess and cling to temporary reliefs;
- follow compulsions;
- intellectualize our emotions;
- win the approval of others by any means necessary;
- project our feelings onto others;
- deny our feelings;
- be narrow-minded;
- procrastinate;
- wait for others to change; or
- seek rewards for good behavior.

Befriending Work: Exploring Unhealthy Defense Mechanisms

Do any of those behaviors seem familiar? Write them down in your journal and briefly describe how each behavior might protect you. I encourage my clients to use plural personal pronouns when giving voice to their protective part. It might sound strange and confusing at first, but when we write "we," we recognize that the protective part tries to convince every part of ourselves to get on board with its defense.

For example, we may identify with fawning or people-pleasing, and then if we tease this behavior out, we may conclude: If we people-please, then we do not have to feel rejected by others. By doing what we believe will make someone else happy, we can avoid feeling ashamed or inadequate.

The Angel and the Devil

When our protective part is not being led well by our Spirit-led adult self, we will experience a lot more confusion, polarization, and inner contention that looks like the classic "angel and devil" iconography. The angel or our Spirit-led adult self will sit on our right shoulder and will say something like, "We need to apologize. We have to be the bigger person. It's the only way we can move forward." The devil, or in this case, our protective part sitting on the left, will say something like, "Heck no! They do not deserve it. Did you see what they did to you?"

If we are prone to ignoring our Spirit-led adult self's voice and are keener to listening to our protective part, we are in for a life of chaos, and we will definitely feel it internally, if not also externally. Unfortunately, this had happened to Jeremiah when he came to see me. Jeremiah could not experience a healthy relationship with a woman and had so much resentment and unforgiveness that he was physically sick. Every day felt miserable. He was barely hanging on by a thread. Jeremiah was unaware that he had gotten so used to listening to his protective part that he couldn't even identify his Spirit-led adult self. Jeremiah's Spirit-led adult self and protective part felt the same.

When we are stuck in survival mode, our primary focus will be to fight off the perceived threat. We will be guided and clouded by our implicit memory, all those traumatic experiences stored in our body, brain, and nervous system that will react to our stressful experiences instead of respond, leaving no room for compassion, love, rest, or even our Spirit-led adult self. Thus, our most intimate relationships, including our relationship with ourselves, begin to suffer.

Covert and Overt Anger

Our protective part can also be quick to anger, including feeling frustration, vengeance, rage, or revenge. This is because anger is motivated by self-protection. Sometimes, we may be so out of touch with our protective part's anger that we do not believe we even have an angry part of ourselves. We may think, "I am not an angry person," or "I have nothing to be angry about," but our anger might not always be apparent. Sometimes our anger is revealed in more covert expressions. Depending on our relationship with anger, we may lean closer to one expression over the other.

Befriending Work: Exploring Your Anger

Take a moment to review this list of covert and overt expressions of anger and jot down in your journal what stands out to you:

- passive-aggressiveness
- jealousy
- sarcasm (which in greek means "flesh-tearing")
- self-sabotage
- stinginess
- hasty generalizations/ judgments
- manipulation
- lying/half-truths
- gaslighting
- skepticism
- bitterness
- self-righteousness
- violent remarks
- loud yelling

- hostility
- disrespect
- ridicule
- betraying others
- provocative language
- visible annoyance
- shifting blame
- revenge
- gossip
- being physically aggressive
- adult "tantrums"
- being overly critical (devaluation)
- stonewalling or becoming distant or withdrawn

As we continue to take an honest look at this part of ourselves, the hope is that we can begin identifying when this protective part comes up in our lives and respond to this part with compassion because, just like our wounded child, our protective part needs lots of it.

Anger Turned Inward, Our Inner Critic

A lot of our protective part's anger is fueled by powerlessness and their own limitations. They often find that their defense mechanisms are no longer protecting the wounded child or there are external forces that are beyond their control. When this happens, we may sense their frustration and annoyance. We may find ourselves feeling tense, heavy, and agitated in our bodies. Sometimes, when our protective part does not know how to protect our wounded child or all of our attempts to alleviate their suffering do not work, our protective part can internalize anger and blame themselves or our adult self. Often this internalization mirrors our caregivers' and important authority figures' criticisms, disparaging remarks, put-downs, and even unhealthy expressions of anger. The harmful voices that have wounded us become our own inner critic to whip us into shape and articulate our unresolved and unexpressed anger. This internal voice often sounds like, "You're an idiot!" "I cannot believe we just did that—what are we thinking?" "Let's just stop while we are ahead—we'll fail!"

Sometimes, the anger is directed to ourselves because our protective part does not feel protected by us. They feel forgotten, alone, or even rejected by us. Consider a teenager who, feeling alone and misunderstood, yells at their parent and says, "I hate you!" Sometimes our protective part, our inner teenager, just wants us to care for them and our wounded child, but they do not know how to share this with us through any other way than beating us down with their words.

The role of this inner critic voice is not meant to hurt us but protect us. Our protective part uses this strategy to move our anger and the underlying frustration with being unable to affect change toward something so disparaging that it will force us to change. For example, when our protective part calls us an idiot, we may work harder to be more careful, and if we are more careful, we may not fail. Or by saying, "You're the worst!"

our protective part might find that we will be more motivated to care for the wounded child. Of course, these protections are distorted and maladaptive, but it is often much safer to turn anger inward than to direct it to someone else.

Often this is what is responsible for our depression. Many renowned psychologists, including Sigmund Freud, saw depression as "anger turned inward." Essentially, when our anger is repressed and directed at ourselves instead of expressed externally, it becomes depression. Dr. Aaron Beck, in his early studies of depression, confirmed this theory in his research with depressed patients. The majority of depressed patients engaged in self-blame, self-criticism, and self-dislike to the point of self-disgust and self-hatred. They were directing their anger inward and beating themselves up in the process.

We also may feel shame for the anger this part of ourselves is holding and the lingering effects it has in our bodies because we may have beliefs or judgments that anger is sinful and forbidden. We may take scripture verses out of context, such as "Refrain from anger, and forsake wrath! Do not fret; it tends only to evil" (Ps 37:8), and we may think, therefore, that we are never allowed to be angry.

Many of us were also harshly reprimanded when we were angry in childhood. We may have been ordered to "go to your room!" or have been accused of being a "brat" or have been told, "You have no right to be angry! Look at how much I have done for you!" These harsh responses weaponize a child's anger and can create an internal message that anger is forbidden and, therefore, unsafe. As a result, children may also hold toxic shame when they begin to feel angry, which is why we may feel an incredible amount of guilt and shame when we feel angry as adults.

The truth is anger and all the other emotions are neither good nor bad. According to the *Catechism of the Catholic Church*, "In the passions (or emotions) as movements of the sensitive appetite, there is neither moral good nor evil. But insofar as they engage reason and will, there is moral good or evil in them" (1773). *Emotion* comes from the Latin word emovere which means "move out." *Emovere* signals that our feelings need to move somewhere and, as we read in the *Catechism of the Catholic Church*, they can help us move toward a moral good.

Remember, when our inner child is an abandoned child, they have not experienced our compassion. The protective part's maladaptive responses are ways of fighting back and reversing the rejection and abandonment every part of us feels. The protective part senses that the wounded child is endangered, and the emotional and physical threats to their self-esteem and dignity become the catalyst for protest and change, even if the protest and change aren't always healthy.

Therefore, we need our protective part's anger and desire to fight back to move us to change unhealthy relationships, systems, situations, or dynamics. We do not need to eradicate this part of ourselves. Instead, we need to take the time to nurture this part and correct them so that they can help us reach a more virtuous end. When reflecting on her protective part, a client of mine shared, "I like my protective self—she is fiery!" At first, I was taken by surprise. I was so used to people struggling to connect with this part of themselves, but I appreciated her sense of ownership for this part of herself because she recognized that it is not bad. Our protective part is a puzzle piece to help us become who we are called to be and, once supported and integrated, become a "fiery" agent to our maturation and healing.

Undetected Anger

Sometimes, the protective part can be more sophisticated, stealthy, and not fiery at all. We may not always detect when our angry child or adolescent self is coming up, especially if we were never allowed to be angry. Thus, our protective part may sound more like this:

> Angel: "We need to set the boundary. It is not okay for her to walk all over you."
> Devil: "No, no. It is okay. We just need to be more careful next time. Let's just avoid her for a couple of weeks."

Another common mental debate that demonstrates the sophisticated ways we have learned to protect ourselves involves procrastination, and it goes something like this:

> Angel: "We need to start this paper. It's due this week."
> Devil: "It's okay. We still have time. Let's watch this show on Netflix instead."

These passive behaviors may go undetected and unidentified as arising from the protective part, but in reality, these passive actions need to be thoroughly examined because they are just as damaging as the more overt, angrily resistant behaviors or self-deprecating self-talk. Passivity is a polite way of saying, "I don't really care about myself too much, and I value protecting myself from judgment from others rather than saying what I really think or feel." Or when it comes to procrastination, "I am so used to living in survival mode that unless I experience a real threat, I have no motivation to do anything that will enhance my well-being." Needless to say, we are still operating from a place of self-abandonment, self-protection, and hidden anger.

Grasping and Clinging

If our protective part does not move from constant self-protection to the loving embrace of God, it will grasp and cling to anyone or anything apart from God. This part of us may instinctively know that it needs help but struggle to know where or from whom to receive it. Therefore, our protective part will end up *emovere*-ing us to something that may offer temporary relief and instant gratification instead of deeper healing. Moving toward more pleasurable feelings can look like being overly attached to a particular person, idea, job, community, or concept. For example, sometimes we can become obsessed with a specific life plan—a vision for our future where everything is idyllic and free from suffering. We can even cling to the idea of the long-awaited "one," the one we are destined to be with and who will complete our lives. It can also look like grasping for material goods or adult security blankets such as new clothes and shoes, seeking the latest technology, having the nicest car, purchasing the biggest house and then constantly renovating and reorganizing it, scrolling on social media, eating an excessive amount of food or restraining oneself from it, or being heavily reliant on sex and its many forms, romantic relationships, drugs, alcohol, and even books, shows, or podcasts.

The problem is that our protective part is under the illusion of control. This part of us grasps and clings to all that cannot satisfy or offer us the healing we need most. Unfortunately, our protective part cannot see this, because it also lives with many unspoken rules that it has been convinced are necessary for our survival. These unspoken rules chain us to the past and keep us from experiencing the Lord's freedom.

Vows and Agreements

Our protective part relies heavily on what Dr. Stephen Porges calls "neuroception," which is our body's neural process that distinguishes environmental and visceral stimuli as safe, dangerous, or life-threatening (Porges, 22–23). Without conscious awareness, this protective part of us constantly works with our neuroception to look for danger cues, especially if they represent anything from our past that brought us pain. When we experience signs of danger, for better or worse, this part of us will spring into action and rely on the unspoken rules to govern our life. Our protective part essentially tells our wounded child, "I am going to make sure you never experience that hurt again."

In Bob Schuchts's work, these same declarations or unspoken rules are referred to as "vows and agreements." He defines vows and agreements as conscious or unconscious decisions to protect ourselves (Schuchts, 118). These vows and agreements are usually connected to a "never," "always," "must," or "cannot" to ensure that we are never wounded again.

Befriending Work: Identifying Vows and Agreements

Take a moment to identify the vows and agreements that your protective part made and write them down in your journal. Here are some common examples:

- We can never trust another person again. If we trust, we will end up getting hurt again.

- We cannot rely on others. We cannot ask for help. We'll just be disappointed.

- We will never express our feelings. They will be used against us.

- We must always put other people's feelings first. Other people matter more than we do.

- We must earn worth and work hard to be lovable. We must please others and make sure everyone is happy with us.

- We cannot fail. If we are struggling it means we need to do more and try harder.

- We must never allow ourselves to feel this pain again. We must always be positive and seek what will offer us pleasurable feelings.

Identifying our vows and agreements can be challenging, especially when we feel powerless over how these unspoken rules create impulsive reactions and lead us to vice, but who knows where we would be without this part of us? This part has been influential in our survival, and now that we are bringing these vows into God's light, we can work with them and turn them into healthy vows and agreements. We will do this in the next chapter.

For example, many clients describe feeling enmeshed with a caregiver or so dominated that they did not experience a unique and separate sense of self. To survive this dysfunctional dynamic, they often learned to be codependent. The threat of rejection and disapproval that came through a parent's loud yelling, frown, glaring eyes, or dismissive body language was enough to spur this part of themselves into doing whatever was necessary to avoid this. Therefore, the protective part led them to adapt to everyone else's needs, to learn to withhold their tongue (their feelings, wants, and desires), and to mold themselves into an image that would offer the wounded child the affirmation, approval, and affection they seek. If the protective part did not do this, they would most likely have been met with rejection, violent outrage, or abuse. Therefore, we can honor our protective part for doing what it believed was necessary for our survival, and we can draw close and offer what this part may need to be set free.

Fear Not, My Child

At the root of our protective part, underneath all of the grasping, clinging, vows, agreements, and anger, is fear. Our protective part, just like the wounded child, is still determining whether or not they will get their deeper needs met. This part of us is terrified of being hurt again, and without the imago dei's light, they are afraid of being consumed by the darkness.

We may also find that other parts of ourselves are afraid of this part too. If you are a parent to a teenager or work with teenagers, you may notice that fear comes up a lot. Teenagers can be full of emotion, resistance, and drama. It can be easy to keep our distance from them or passively give in to their demands. But if we treat our protective part in the same way and see them as a "scary teenager," we run the risk of them controlling our adult life. Therefore, as we draw closer to the wounded child's fear, we must also draw near to our protective part's fear. Our protective part is not a scary teenager but often a teen part of ourselves that is terrified. And just like every teenager, this part needs our mercy and compassion. It needs to be understood. It cries out, "Someone, please hear me! See me! Understand me! Help me!"

One of my favorite stories in the Bible that illustrates our protective part is when Jesus is with Mary and Martha. Mary sits at Jesus's feet. She can rest in her imago dei as she recognizes God in her presence. However, Martha is busy with all the preparation. We can imagine Martha frantically moving about the home, cooking, cleaning, and ensuring that everyone is happy. Then we hear Martha complain, "Lord, do you not care that my sister has left me to serve alone? Tell her then to help me" (Lk 10:40). Martha is guided by her protective part. The angry little girl or adolescent within her demands justice. She wants to make things "right." She sees keeping busy and ensuring that everyone is okay as the appropriate responses to protect her wounded child from rejection, abandonment, or invalidation. Perhaps she thinks that if she does not do this, Jesus would be upset with her. He would say she is a poor host. He would leave the home and go away. To her surprise, however, Jesus doesn't do any of this but invites her to lower her defense.

"Martha, Martha," the Lord answers, "you are anxious and troubled about many things; one thing is needful. Mary has chosen the good portion, which shall not be taken away from her" (Lk 10:41–42). Resting, surrendering, moving away from our self-reliance, and seeing our need for Jesus is the better way, and that is what we have to help our protective part see too. As we look to Jesus to do this, we see God is not afraid of our anger, self-protection, defenses, and inner vows and agreements. Therefore, we can take courage and help this part to experience the love and support they need. We want this part of ourselves to experience safety and let God protect and heal this part of us, along with our wounded child.

If we allow this part of ourselves to run the show, we can get to a place where we work so hard to protect that we begin to crumble under the weight of it all. Our protective part shuts down and can become helpless, hopeless, quick to procrastinate, lethargic, and even depressed (the anger turned inward), which puts us back into a dorsal shutdown state or hypoarousal.

The protective part adopts a learned helplessness mindset. This part of us begins to believe that nothing seems to work, so we might as well give up and stop trying. If Martha did not let this part cry out, she might not have been able to truly be heard. She may have collapsed in the kitchen under the weight of all the pressure she was carrying and allowed herself to grow in anger, bitterness, resentment, hopelessness, and despair. Fortunately, just like Martha, we can cry out, too, and trust that Jesus hears our cries and the Holy Spirit can mobilize us toward proper action again. We can move from a place of learned helplessness into learned optimism.

"Learned optimism" is a term coined by the American psychologists Steven Maier and Martin Seligman. Their research revealed that the only way humans can move through helplessness is to explain the events to themselves constructively and develop a positive internal dialogue (Maier and Seligman). We can apply this to our protective part and support its pleas, protests, anger, fear, mistrust, and even despondency by developing a trusting relationship with this part.

Our protective part is a prominent skeptic, so building a trusting relationship will not be easy. This part of us holds much of our lack of faith, especially with Jesus and other authority figures. They can even be responsible for our struggle to pray, receive the sacraments, or do what we know can be helpful for our healing. They are simply afraid that these people, institutions, practical strategies, or even gifts from the Church will let us down, just like the people who have let down the wounded child. So, when we start with "You are going to be okay; let go and let God," we might notice the protective part's frustration or resistance. We must begin by offering what will support this part's *felt sense* of safety and security instead of a cognitive understanding that they can trust us.

This part begins to soften once they feel truly seen, heard, and supported. We may feel our clenched fists and jaws release or our chest feeling lighter. When this happens, a seed of trust is planted that we can viscerally feel. Then, cognitive understanding follows. This part of ourselves begins to think, "Maybe I can surrender." "Maybe there is someone who will support me." "Maybe the wounded child will be okay without me having to work so hard to protect them." This curious wondering moves the part closer to healing and wholeness.

Healing Is a Process

I wish I could tell you that Jeremiah, from the beginning of this chapter, no longer feels angry—that he is full of joy and peace and can rest—but this would not be true or realistic. Jeremiah is still working with his protective part and learning to give that part of himself what they need. Jeremiah recognizes that his protective part doesn't budge easily and has many vows and agreements that will take supernatural grace to lift. But here's where the hope comes in. Jeremiah is free. He chooses healing and wholeness. He does not let this fragmented part run the show. Instead, he consciously tries to befriend this terrified, mistrusting, and angry part of himself.

Jeremiah also does not shame or condemn his protective part's feelings. Instead, he makes room for these feelings, identifies when this part is being prideful and leading him to sin, and gently brings this part of himself to the Sacrament of Reconciliation. Jeremiah also works to soften this part through prayer, the support of a good friend, and weekly Eucharistic Adoration. He tells his protective part, "I will be patient with you. You are deserving of my love and care." In other words, he does not abandon this part of himself.

As we strive to meet our protective part's needs, we recognize that our protective part needs our leadership, and with our leadership, we can break cycles of conflict, suffering, and opposition. Therefore, we cannot label this part as "bad" or "good" or judge how this part has learned to protect us. We just need to draw near, and as we do, in this lifetime or the next, this part of us will look a lot like the imago dei and a lot like God.

What once was fragmented and cut away from our imago dei can now become an active agent in our healing process. Our protective part can support us in reclaiming our wholeness so that our imago dei shines again and our Spirit-led adult self can lead.

Prayer

Father, I thank you for creating my body in a way that helps me survive. I am starting to recognize my protective part, and I am understanding how it seeks to support me and my wounded child. Help me to remain curious and draw near to this part's anger, defensiveness, mistrust, vows and agreements, and fear, as you also draw near to this part, Father, so that this part of me can experience your healing. Amen.

Befriending Work: Exploring Your Protective Part Further

- Find a picture of yourself that best represents a time in your life when you were stuck in survival mode or experiencing a lot of anger, mistrust, or pride. Reflect on and pray with this image this week.

- How was anger expressed in your childhood? How did people respond to you when you were angry? How do you want to express anger now as an adult?

- Write a letter to your protective part, sharing your hopes and desires for this part of you.

Guided Meditation

To listen to my guided meditation for this chapter, scan the QR code below or go to https://www.avemariapress.com/befriending-inner-child-meditations.

5

Stepping into Your Spirit-Led Adult Self

When I left the transformational therapy session I described in chapter 1, I had this strange desire to listen to "Lucky" by Britney Spears. It was a song I really loved when I was a child, but a song I had forgotten all about as an adult. I searched for it on Spotify and hit play and listened intently to the lyrics, hoping for any clues that would tell me more about my child self. Suddenly, all the words and feelings attached to the song came rushing back to my memory. As Britney's voice traveled through my speakers, I belted the lyrics out loud in an off-key pitch and bobbed my head with the melody. It did not take long until I suddenly started laughing to myself and then crying simultaneously. I felt so ridiculous singing an old Britney Spears song in my car and then breaking out in tears, yet I held a tremendous amount of compassion for my child self. I could recall my child self listening to this song on her Walkman, singing along and feeling sad but not knowing why.

For the first time, I was an adult willing to care for myself in a way that went deeper than warm bubble baths, hikes, and a trip to the nail salon. I was drawing closer to what was unhealed, crying out, and needing support within me. I was becoming more curious and allowing myself to make space for the feelings accompanying my discoveries. I was beginning the journey of befriending my inner child and no longer being led by child parts but by my adult self.

Our North Star

We all have an adult self who has been created to rise above what is wounded and fractured and bring healing. From the moment of our conception, we have been given this part to repair our fragmentation. Our adult self cooperates with God's plan for our healing and restoration. As they develop their God-given intellect and use their free will, they become an active participant in God's redemption so that every part of us bears the image and likeness of God.

The *Catechism of the Catholic Church* states, "The human person participates in the light and power of the divine Spirit. . . . By free will, he is capable of directing himself toward his true good. He finds his perfection 'in seeking and loving what is true and good.' By virtue of his soul and his spiritual powers of intellect and will, man is endowed with freedom, an 'outstanding manifestation of the divine image'" (CCC, 1704–5). In other words, our adult self is like the North Star within us. They point us back to God and help us to live as beloved children of God. When we let this part lead and give them power and authority over the other parts, we can move closer to who we truly are and the plan God has for each of us. We live a life that radiates God's goodness, and our child parts are ushered closer to our heavenly home.

Where Our Adult Self Lives

From a nervous system and brain science perspective, our adult self lives in our prefrontal cortex, the part of our brain responsible for decision-making, moderating social behavior, and executive function. When our prefrontal cortex is activated, it engages with our social engagement system or ventral vagal state, which, if you remember from the previous chapters, is the state that helps us experience our imago dei. The more we activate our prefrontal cortex and bring regulation to our nervous system, the more our adult self can take root and direct our inner child to the true, good, and beautiful.

Our inner child may see and experience the true, good, and beautiful but often cannot consciously choose it. They are led by their emotions and self-interests. As we saw with our wounded child, they quickly become confused and internalize their experiences. They do not have the emotional regulation and cognitive ability to sort their experiences and stay rooted in their belovedness. Our protective part can be easily angered and rush into self-protection without weighing the consequences or tempering emotions, thus losing sight of what is important and more virtuous.

The A.D.U.L.T. Self

Our adult self is the only part capable of being an A.D.U.L.T. because it is the only part capable of the following:

- Accepting
- Disciplining
- Understanding
- Loving
- Tending

Let's explore this acronym, letter by letter.

Accepting

To live as an adult, we must be willing to accept that there are some things we cannot change and control. Our fractured child parts do not understand this. They often desperately yearn for something they believe is in their grasp—a parent to affirm them, justice for something unfair, or to be good enough finally in the eyes of another.

Our adult self knows that to live an integrated life, they must stop clinging, grasping, and fighting. They must live a life of acceptance. In grief work, acceptance is the final task. We work through denial, anger, bargaining, longing, avoidance, and depression to get to where we can say with faith and hope.

> Behold, God is my salvation;
> I will trust, and will not be afraid;
> for the LORD God is my strength and my song,
> and he has become my salvation. (Is 12:2)

Our adult self recognizes that to experience this profound trust, they will have to come face-to-face with what they lost or with what our protective part is afraid of losing. Perhaps it is the loss of important people who died too soon or were not there to care for us, the loss of missed developmental milestones, the loss of unmet needs, and perhaps even the loss of our inner child. Or maybe for our protective part it is the loss of no longer running the show.

If we do not allow ourselves to work through the loss and get to a place of acceptance, our inner child will often hold on to disordered attachments that keep us from experiencing the fullness of God and the fullness of our being. In *Introduction to Christianity*, Cardinal Joseph Ratzinger (Pope Benedict XVI) wrote, "Man comes in the profoundest sense to himself, not through what he does, but through what he accepts" (Ratzinger, 223). Therefore, we must discover how to practice healthy detachment and surrender what is beyond our limitations, which includes healing our own self completely, being loved by others in the way we desire, changing the past and the effects it has on our present, preventing future harm, and earning our own worth. Here, in our surrendering and acceptance, we discover true freedom. We learn how to be secure adults, trusting and abiding in God.

Disciplining

Children do not have discipline. *Discipline* comes from the Latin word *disciplina*, meaning "instruction, education, or training." It is where we get the word *disciple*. Children must be taught discipline, and adults are the only ones capable of teaching it. When adults are disciplined, they can better teach and train their children. Adolescents are often frustrated with their parents because of the disorder they see in their discipline. "It all seems so unfair!" is a common declaration. A parent may tell their teenage daughter, "Don't you talk to me with that tone!" by screaming at them, or "You're grounded for two weeks!" without any explanation.

Our adult self must grow in self-discipline to instruct and better lead our inner child and respond to God's love and his holy will. Healthy discipline that is modeled well helps our inner child trust in our adult self's leadership. Consider the twelve apostles. Jesus gave them healthy discipline. Order and balance were present. They knew who was in charge. They knew the rules and the consequences of breaking those rules. They knew when to pray, sleep, move to the next city, stay awake, and engage with those they encountered. They were prompted to delay gratification and sacrifice for the greater good. Without discipline, chaos would have ensued. The apostles would have done whatever they each wanted. The demands of others would have heavily burdened them. They would have felt entitled and more special than others. They would have been more prone to pride and self-sufficiency, which we see Jesus corrects repeatedly in scripture so that his followers can grow in maturity.

St. Paul writes in his Letter to the Corinthians, "When I was a child, I spoke like a child, I thought like a child, I reasoned like a child; when I became a man, I gave up childish ways" (1 Cor 13:11). Giving up impulsivity, self-centeredness, emotional reasoning, and entitlement is a part of moving from thinking and reasoning like a child to becoming an adult. Therefore, to grow in self-discipline we also will have to grow in understanding.

Understanding

Understanding blossoms as we learn and become more conscious. When we understand why we do what we do, think what we think, feel what we feel, process our story, and uncover our needs, wants, and desires, we become aware of what will help our fractured inner child heal, and we better love them. As Proverbs reminds us, "He who gets wisdom loves himself; he who keeps understanding will prosper" (19:8). Our adult self is the only part capable of understanding because they are the only one that can truly discern the meaning of things. This means the adult self can help us resolve what we discover within ourselves and bring integration. They can also help us better understand others, increasing our capacity to care for others and forgive offenses.

Understanding also helps us to be more creative and flexible thinkers. It moves us from black-and-white and all-or-nothing thinking so that we can embrace complexity. We can resolve our cognitive dissonance, the clashing thoughts within our mind, and our actions that seem to be at war with what we know to be true. Through understanding, we can also become more curious about what we are experiencing and how our inner child may need us to respond. We can be more compassionate and extend mercy to those most in need.

To accomplish this, we must learn how to grow our understanding of God and how God views us so that "we may no longer be children, tossed back and forth and carried about with every wind of doctrine, by the cunning of men, by their craftiness in deceitful wiles" (Eph 4:14). This can look like meditating on God's word in scripture, developing stronger prayer habits, being active in a church community, receiving the sacraments, hanging around people who are close to God, or reading spiritual or theological books.

One of the best things I have done to help my adult self step into leadership is to read more books. Reading books on parenting, psychology, Church doctrine, and the lives of the saints has helped me understand what I have yet to discover within me and become more confident in how I care for the parts of myself. I have also found praying the Liturgy of the Hours or Divine Office helpful. The Liturgy of the Hours is a structure for daily prayer that offers us an opportunity to participate in the life of the Church at various points throughout the day and "pray constantly" (1 Thes 5:17). Morning, Midafternoon, Afternoon, Evening, and Night Prayer can help us meditate on the mystery of God from the moment we awake to the moment we go to sleep. As I read the daily readings, psalms, and petitions for the day, I begin to understand God's heart. I also have more structure in my day, which helps me to stay committed to prayer.

The more we increase our knowledge of God and his presence in us, the more we increase our security. We develop the understanding that will keep us from being manipulated and led by our raw emotions, faulty beliefs, or youthful passions and, as a result, support our inner child to feel safe, deeply understood, and loved.

Loving

Children can be very loving, but their love is often conditional. Children usually behave more lovingly if they receive what they want, but once we remove something they want, they may kick, scream, pout, hide, or turn away. Children have to mature in their love.

The adult self can teach children how to love maturely because the adult self is constantly growing in love. As this part "puts away childish things," they can think, talk, and respond in a way that can begin to reflect God's unconditional love. The adult self can is also accomplish this through sacrifice—a core tenant of love. In St. Paul's Letter to the Ephesians, he tells us, "Therefore be imitators of God, as beloved children. And walk in love, as Christ loved us and gave himself up for us, a fragrant offering and sacrifice to God" (5:1–2). Often, instead of leaning into God's example of healing love, we are tempted to follow the negative example of our caregiver, the bully in third grade, or the teacher in middle school who never really believed in us.

The absence of love and poor examples of love in our youth become a template for withholding or expressing love conditionally. We may also hold unspoken beliefs about love that are far from the way Christ loves us, but as Christians, we are always called to a higher form of thinking and loving. Therefore, the adult self has to love without counting the cost. They must love sacrificially and, with that sacrifice, make difficult decisions, refrain from wants and desires for a higher good, and seek what is best for our inner child and what is best for others. It also must offer repair and forgive others "seventy times seven" times (Mt 18:22).

Forgiveness can be very challenging for our protective part. Sometimes when our adult self desires to forgive, our protective part will step in to keep us from actually doing it. Our protective part is often convinced that it cannot forgive unless there is retribution or reconciliation. Therefore, our adult self must step in to support our protective part in surrendering and forgiving because, as we see through Jesus's discipleship and ministry, it is the only way to truly love and tend to ourselves and others well.

Tending

Tending means anticipating needs and then compassionately meeting those needs. As stated in chapter 4, the protective part can develop earned security and tend to our inner child in ways that we may have never experienced before.

When our adult self is running the show, they will tend to every part of us. They will move closer to the wounded child's hurts, fears, disappointment, longing, sadness, and unmet needs and the protective part's resistance, anger, frustration, fears, and desires. They will delight in our imago dei and make space for our talents, gifts, and passions. The adult self will also tend to our body and respond to our body's needs: food, drink, rest, connection, warmth, and so on, as well as tend to our spiritual needs: Reconciliation, prayer, fasting, the Eucharist, connection to God, and so on.

As our adult self tends to our inner child's needs well, the expectation or hope that we will get our needs met by our caregivers is released. Psychologist Carl Jung writes in *Psychology and Alchemy*, "No matter how much the parents and grandparents may have sinned against the child, the man who is really adult will accept these sins as his own condition which has to be reckoned with" (115).

Our adult self recognizes that they are now responsible for ensuring that their needs are met and recognizes that those who have failed them reflect our imperfect human condition, which we must reconcile with God. Failure to release our expectations and hopes that our caregivers or spouse, friends, community, government, or Church will heal us puts us in a perpetual state of desperation and defense. We cannot tend to anyone or anything well because we constantly search for something that only God can provide.

Therefore, tending is our responsibility, and when we become more responsible and responsive to our fractured parts, we can begin supporting them in ways others couldn't or won't. We move from fight or flight to what Shelley Taylor and colleagues call "tend and befriend" (Taylor, 32–49).

To tend and befriend is an adaptive response. It recognizes that our survival does not have to be one of eradicating our wounds or becoming more self-reliant to heal them. In our stress, we can respond in a way that protects and cares for our inner child, the most vulnerable within us, while also moving from merely surviving (fight, flight, freeze, fawn) to thriving and connecting.

Guided by the Holy Spirit

We must recognize that even when we A.D.U.L.T. well, our best attempts to tend and befriend our fractured parts will be limited. There will still be a block to reclaiming and becoming all that we have been created to be. The only way our adult self can truly bring parts into integration and experience deeper healing and wholeness is through the love and guidance of the Holy Spirit.

The Holy Spirit is the greatest resource God has given us to restore our wholeness. God knew that we could not reclaim our wholeness and experience deep healing without him. In John's gospel, Jesus says, "If you love me, you will keep my commandments. And I will ask the Father, and he will give you another Counselor, to be with you forever, even the Spirit of truth, whom the world cannot receive, because it neither sees him nor knows him; you know him, for he dwells with you, and will be in you"(14:15–17). Therefore, when we allow our adult self to be led by the Holy Spirit, the Holy Spirit helps us, dwells in us, and keeps us tethered to our triune God. As the Holy Spirit animates our whole being, we allow ourselves to be fathered by God, to participate in Christ's redemption, and to live in spirit and truth. We are given the "power and love and self-control" that moves us toward right action (2 Tm 1:7), and in our movement toward right action, we experience unification. We are no longer fractured and disintegrated, but every part is living as God's beloved again because "where the Spirit of the Lord is, there is freedom" to become all that we were made to be (2 Cor 3:17). We are free to become children of God (see Romans 8:14–17).

Sometimes, we think we won't be free and able to live our God-given identity until we no longer experience our wounded child or our protective part never springs into action to protect us in a maladaptive way anymore. What makes us truly free to be God's child, however, is not the absence of our wounds and self-protection but the ability to respond to our wounds and self-protection with love. Through the Holy Spirit, we are given several gifts to accomplish this. All we have to do is choose to use them.

The Gifts of the Holy Spirit

The gifts I am referring to are the gifts of the Holy Spirit. They are Christ's virtuous characteristics, which Christ freely shares with us as God's children. These gifts are infused into all of us at Baptism. They are also nurtured in the domestic church (our families) and sealed in the Sacrament of Confirmation. These gifts help us to live with dual awareness. We can recognize our human limitations and imperfection, including what we discover within our fractured parts, and yet simultaneously transcend so that we can see ourselves through the eyes of God.

According to Catholic tradition, the seven gifts of the Holy Spirit are understanding, counsel, knowledge, wisdom, piety, fear of God, and fortitude. I will offer a short description of each gift and how we can use them to reclaim our wholeness and experience healing for our inner child. I invite you to pause, reflect on each one, and notice what comes up for you as you read through.

Understanding

Understanding helps us to think clearly, perceive, comprehend, interpret information, and have insight to discern meaning. For example, when we notice an internal war within us, we might use the gift of understanding to try to interpret what part may be coming up and what our parts may need. Usually, our healing journey will begin with understanding. We will notice parts of ourselves come up, and we will begin to get curious about them and perhaps even seek additional counsel.

Counsel

Counsel helps us to be directed by God through sound advice, teaching, useful information, warning, recommendations, and encouragement. It includes giving good counsel to others as well. When we are unsure how to support a particular part, we may seek wise counsel. We may turn to a psychotherapist, spiritual director, or trusted confidant and ask for advice. Upon seeking counsel on our healing journey, we typically will grow in self-knowledge.

Knowledge

Knowledge helps us to judge correctly. Through knowledge, we can study, learn, retain, and master facts and information and use what is learned to make difficult decisions and discern well. For example, we may feel called to pursue a particular vocation, but our wounded child may feel afraid because they do not want to experience rejection, and our protective part may then want to avoid the vocation in an effort to protect the wounded child from rejection. Knowledge helps us pursue our vocation, work through our parts' feelings, and rely on what we know to be true. As we continue to apply our knowledge, our wisdom will increase.

Wisdom

Wisdom helps us exercise good judgment, distinguish between right and wrong, and uphold truth and justice. When we experience our protective part's yearning for justice, we can use wisdom to help us navigate how to fight for justice and truth, all while respecting other people's free will. Or when we experience our wounded child, we can use wisdom to help us understand why they are feeling certain feelings, where those feelings come from, and how to respond to them. As our wisdom continues to expand, so will our piety.

Piety

Piety helps us to develop personal holiness. It is our devotion to God, prayer, virtue, goodness, self-mastery, and the ability to avoid sin and obey God's will even when we do not feel like it. For example, when we feel overwhelmed by our fractured inner child, we may pray to God. Instead of letting overwhelming feelings lead us to immature or inappropriate self-soothing, medicating, or abandoning, we can use the gift of piety to turn to a higher good such as going to Eucharistic Adoration, journaling, walking in nature, and so on. As our personal holiness becomes more and more rooted, so will our fear of God.

Fear of God

Fear of God helps us to have the utmost respect for God. It is how we can experience awe and reverence and recognize God in all things. It also allows us to move from seeking validation and security in others toward confidence in God, and it helps us gladly offer praise and adoration to God, even when we are suffering. For example, when we are experiencing the wounds of our wounded child and their pain is not going away, we still proclaim the goodness of God. When our fear of God becomes our motivation, strength, and hope, we will then have the fortitude to continue in this work, no matter what obstacles we are presented with in the future.

Fortitude

Fortitude helps us to be steadfast. It is how we can avoid evil and self-sufficiency, and when faced with adversity, we can experience courage, determination, patient endurance, and resiliency. For example, when we support the integration of our parts, fortitude will help us to be patient with them and "suffer with" them. It will help us not to grow weary or worry about how long it is taking to heal and instead persevere. We can stay committed to befriending our inner child.

Come, Holy Spirit!

Therefore, as we invite the Holy Spirit in to guide and sustain our adult self, we are able to accomplish more than we ever thought we could be capable of:

- We will put on the mind of Christ Jesus. We will experience the "helper who will teach us all things and bring into our memory everything that Jesus has proclaimed" (Jn 14:26).

- We will not be conformed to this world. We will be transformed. Our minds will be renewed (including how we have learned to think, protect ourselves, understand our traumatic memories, and see ourselves, God, and others). We will discern the will of God well and choose "what is good and acceptable and perfect" (Rom 12:2).

- We will become new people. We will reclaim our being made in the image and likeness of God and experience holiness and wholeness (see Ephesians 4:24).

- We also will attain unity of faith and knowledge of God. We become mature adults "to the measure of the stature of the fulness of Christ" (Eph 4:13).

When we invite the Holy Spirit into our lives, the Spirit radiates within us and fills every gap of our internal fracture. As a result, we experience the fruits of the Holy Spirit: self-control, patience, joy, peace, love, gentleness, generosity, faithfulness, and kindness—everything that makes life worth living! If we do not see these fruits in our life, it is possible that our wounded child or protective part is leading us. When this happens, we will have to rely on the Holy Spirit and integrative practices to help us get back into our adult selves even more. We will explore this more in part 2.

Jesus, Our Model and Guide

Learning how to live guided by the Holy Spirit and become a Spirit-led adult self can also be accomplished through modeling ourselves after Jesus. Jesus is the ultimate Spirit-led adult. There is no division within him. He is unified and whole, and because of that, he can reveal to us what it looks like to be a mature adult who can bring unification to our internal fracture.

For those of us who have experienced complex trauma, we may have not seen many mature behaviors modeled, which can make it more challenging to be a Spirit-led adult self and look to Jesus. We may think that Jesus's mature behaviors are too holy or too far from what we are capable of. Although Jesus is holy and will always show us a more perfect way than we can muster up ourselves, we can actually grow in ways that look a lot like Jesus. There is nothing that Jesus showed us that we cannot mirror in some way as we practice becoming a Spirit-led adult self and experiencing the healing effects of it.

In fact, brain science reveals that our brains have neuro-plasticity, which means our brains can change and adapt with experience. We can grow new neural pathways, create new connections, and in some cases, even create new neurons. A common phrase used within psychology, "Neurons that fire together, rewire together," points to this incredible gift of adaptation. As we learn new things about Jesus, expand our awareness about how he loves, experience a healthy relationship with him, and process our experiences with him, we can take care of our minds, bodies, and souls alongside Jesus.

Living by Your New ABCs

It is from this place of deep relationship with the Trinity that we can begin showing up for our inner child in ways we never could imagine. We can participate in God's redemptive healing, reclaim the wholeness Christ already won for us through the Cross, and live our new ABCs.

The second part of this book is all about these ABCs. The *A*'s are my five-step process for inner child work. We will learn how to *anchor, acknowledge, attune, ask,* and *act* so that we can become more rooted in our Holy Spirit–led adult self and practice our *B*'s—*befriending* our inner child and *becoming* more like Christ—and as a result, grow in our *C*'s: developing *curiosity, compassion, clarity, connectedness, creativity, courage, confidence,* and *calm.*

I am fond of these C's from Dr. Richard Schwartz's internal family systems theory because they reflect the traits of our imago dei and our Spirit-led adult self. As we rely on the gifts of the Holy Spirit and experience the fruits of the Holy Spirit, we will see our adult self become more integrated with our fractured parts, and as a result, we will experience our imago dei more profoundly in our lives. We will become one with our authentic core and with God.

As we become more one with our authentic core and with God, we can be *curious* about the world around us and whatever we discover within us. We can hold *compassion* for ourselves and others. We can move from confusion to *clarity* about who we really are. We can feel *connected* to God, ourselves, and others. We can be *creative* in the face of challenge and adversity and become cocreators of a better world. We can be *courageous* when faced with the unknown and our deepest fears. We can be *confident* that we are not abandoned and that God will be with us always, and we can feel *calm* and at peace in God's providence and care.

We also will find that the unspoken vows and agreements that have governed our life for so long will change. We will experience new inner vows and agreements that will bring us safety, security, and peace and increase the three theological virtues—faith, hope, and love—in us.

Befriending Work: Declaring Healthy Vows and Agreements

Take a moment to reflect on what new, healthy vows and agreements you want to lead with. Think of them as your new personal commandments and what you are giving your fractured inner child permission to do to heal and become whole. Here are some examples:

- It can be safe to be in an intimate relationship with other people. We no longer have to hide ourselves. We can show up authentically.

- It is okay to ask for help. We can get support from others to get our needs met.

- We do not have to be the savior. We have a Savior to trust in and bring others to. We can rest and allow ourselves to be taken care of.

Our new vows and agreements will help us live with personal integrity and personal boundaries that will allow us to respect who we are and nurture who we have been created to become. It may also be helpful to review your core beliefs from chapter 3 and reclaim the truth of who you are by challenging each belief with who God says you are. For example, your wounded child may have a core belief that says, "I am not enough." As you sit with this belief and ask God, "Who do you say that I am?" God may reveal to you, "You are my child–you are enough!"

Now, try declaring your new vows and agreements, including your new core beliefs, out loud. Imagine Jesus standing beside you and every part of you before you: your imago dei, wounded child, and protective part. Give them the freedom to be who they were created to be.

More often than not, our fractured child parts are just waiting for strong and compassionate leadership. They are waiting for someone authentic, patient, and resourced enough to give them safety, security, and permission to live out what trauma, sin, wounding, and grief convinced them they could not do or could not become. We can be that person our inner child needs. Through the Holy Spirit alive in us, through God's gifts of our intellect and will, and through the example of our compassionate Lord, we have the power to support our inner child to become God's whole child. "Behold, now is the acceptable time; behold, now is the day of salvation" (2 Cor 6:2). This is the day of our healing. This is the day for wholeness. This is the day for reclaiming and becoming.

Prayer

Father, I thank you for the mature adult self you are molding me into. I thank you for sending me your Spirit and allowing me to partake in the gifts and fruits of the Holy Spirit that bring healing and integration to my inner child. You have not abandoned me, and I trust that you will continue to guide me and help me to become more and more like you. Amen.

Befriending Work: Exploring Your Spirit-Led Adult Self Further

• What qualities, traits, virtues, or spiritual gifts does your adult self possess? When and where do you typically see your Spirit-led adult self lead?

• Write down your triggers or the challenges that may make it harder for your Spirit-led adult self to lead. See if you can be more mindful when presented with these triggers or challenges, so you can call on the name of the Holy Spirit and step into your adult self.

• What gifts of the Holy Spirit can you pray for more so you can live more guided by the Holy Spirit? What fruits of the Holy Spirit are you seeing or would like to see more of in your life right now?

Guided Meditation

To listen to my guided meditation for this chapter, scan the QR code below or go to https://www.avemariapress.com/befriending-inner-child-meditations.

Part 2

Drawing Near to Your Inner Child

6

Anchor

Layloni sought therapy to address a pervasive feeling of anxiety that she could not fully explain. She was enjoying marriage, loving her career, and experiencing peace in her family of origin, but she could not shake this unsettling fear and anxiousness that lived in her body.

When we explored where this anxiety may have come from, Layloni shared that it could be from an abusive relationship that began in high school and that ended during her senior year of college. Layloni described how she had walked on eggshells during this relationship, not knowing when her partner would flip his lid. She was often blamed for extenuating circumstances and manipulated into believing she was powerless and stuck in the relationship. It made sense why Layloni would believe that this relationship had flared her anxiety, but as she continued to speak and dive deeper into her childhood, I identified a reason far more common. Layloni had lost her anchor.

An anchor is an object that attaches a ship or boat to the bottom of a body of water. It allows the boat to remain steady and not drift away with the winds and waves. For first-century Christians, an anchor was the symbol of Christianity. It was the promise and hope of Christ. No matter what we experience in this life, we can be assured, "We have this as a sure and steadfast anchor of the soul, a hope" (Heb 6:19).

As God's children, we can go through difficult experiences, endure painful relationships, and even become confused by the anomalies in life, and yet, when we have a strong and secure anchor, we are not swept away by any of this. The anchor keeps us firm and secure, able to regulate our bodies, make healthy decisions such as walking away from a harmful relationship, and hold fast to the truth. It gives us agency and abounding hope.

For many years, Layloni believed her anchor was God. She went to Catholic school, was raised in a Catholic home, married in the Catholic Church, and regularly practiced her Catholic faith, but we had come to find that her faith was more like a security blanket. Instead of it connecting her closer to the Divine Healer, it was more of a soft cover that hid her deepest fears. When her security blanket no longer gave her warm and comforting feelings, Layloni felt lost, confused, anxious, and depressed. Many of us can find ourselves in a similar place. We believe in God and the Church and have receipts to prove we have done all the right things; however, we find that when we have lost our sense of security or safety, when we no longer feel okay, we are not truly allowing God to anchor us.

When Layloni and I explored her childhood in-depth, we unearthed her fragmenting four—the sin, trauma, attachment injuries, and complicated grief she endured, which started way before the abusive relationship she was in. Many of her negative beliefs about herself, including her lack of a sense of agency, did not come from her ex-boyfriend but stemmed from little experiences throughout her childhood. Fortunately, Layloni was not abused, physically threatened, or neglected within her family of origin. She never witnessed her parents argue or anything that frightened her to her core, but she did experience "death by a million paper cuts."

Layloni was the youngest of three, and there was a significant age gap between her and her two older siblings, which often left her feeling alone, disconnected, and unimportant. Layloni learned from these experiences that her voice and opinion did not matter. She also could not recall times when her parents asked her how she felt or asked her opinion on a particular topic. Layloni's entire emotional world was often chalked up to the label "she's just too sensitive."

So, although her family practiced their faith and sent her to Catholic school, and although she had been active in her faith, when Layloni started to experience heavier winds and waves as a teenager, they completely rocked her. She may have desired God to be her anchor, but the God she had in mind was not real. It was a counterfeit God who looked much like her parents and siblings. A God who was not too interested in the details of her life. A God who could abandon her in her darkest hour and see her as being "too sensitive." A God who did not care to hear her voice and bypassed her feelings.

Without an anchor capable of keeping her grounded, Layloni could not stay rooted in her imago dei. She unconsciously believed she had to rely on herself because that was the only person her protective part told her she could really have faith in. As a result, she developed a heightened state of arousal to protect herself from any perceived threat, and when she was in her abusive relationship, that heightened state of arousal only went into hyperdrive, which prevented her from experiencing the beauty and goodness in her life and robbed her of internal peace.

Hold On to Me

In her song "My Anchor," Christy Nockels repeats the words, "Jesus, I hold on to You, and You hold on to me." This is what happens when our anchor is in God. We can reach out with trust and hold on to him and believe he will hold on to us. He won't let us go.

We may think that our anchor is our dog, cat, nature, music, daily Mass, the Rosary, prayer, or our children, best friend, or spouse, but the deeper truth is that our anchor is God alive and present with us through these people, animals, activities, and things we do and are in relationship with.

God is our true anchor: God the Father, Son, and Holy Spirit. We must recognize that if we fail to see God in what grounds us and let God be our anchor, anything we use to replace him won't have the ability and full capacity to hold on to us the way we need to be held.

Therefore, seeing God as our true anchor helps us to stay planted. It keeps us firm and secure and living more in the image and likeness of God. It helps us to support our inner child consistently without being carried away by our current stressors, struggles, triggers, and distressing feelings. With God, we can be rooted in the promise and hope of being loved and cared for endlessly.

With God as our anchor, we can also stay more grounded in our ventral vagal state. Our social engagement system is more easily activated, and we can simultaneously experience our imago dei and our Spirit-led adult self more readily. We typically experience this viscerally when our body feels steady, the pains and pressure we often carry in our bodies are released, our muscles feel loose, our facial expressions are soft, and our heart is slowed down in a steady rhythm. This is a peaceful place to be in. We are not overwhelmed, burned out, anxious, sad, overstimulated, hypervigilant, overreacting, or on edge, but we are allowing our inner child to be rocked back and forth in God's loving arms.

We also are not blended with our parts. Being "blended" is a term developed by Dr. Richard Schwartz in internal family systems therapy (24). When parts are blended, it is difficult to distinguish the child from the adult, and without a regulated and anchored adult, our wounded or protective inner child takes control. We saw this with Jeremiah. He had no idea how to regulate his body, and he didn't know who was his inner child and who was his adult self. When this happens internally, it will be difficult to tend to our inner child because in the sea of competing voices, wants, needs, and feelings, we will experience utter chaos and disintegration that keep our Spirit-led adult self from being in leadership.

Without the adult self's leadership, we cannot be anchored. Children cannot remain anchored without the care and support of a loving adult, which is why our anchoring must include internal boundaries that help our inner child know that we are allowed to feel our feelings, voice our thoughts, and have a negative reaction to experiences and people; yet, our Spirit-led adult self runs the show. Our parts cannot break the healthier vows and agreements that our Spirit-led adult self has made.

Consider a family who has a child with high needs. That child will take up a lot of space in the family, and rightfully so.

They are in need. However, if there are not boundaries, structure, or an adult to bring order, chaos will ensue. Over time,
the family will fall apart, and nobody's needs will be tended
to. We must think of our internal world similarly: as an overwhelmed family who needs a loving and attentive adult who
has resources and leadership to tend to the child's high needs.

We can be the adult who provides the love and attention
our inner child needs when we become unblended so that we
can remain anchored in God. Through the inspiration and
guidance of the Holy Spirit, the care of our heavenly Father,
and the example and friendship of Jesus, along with practical
coping strategies and resources, we can make tough decisions,
set boundaries, and provide discipline that helps us stay rooted
in our imago dei and thus rooted in God.

Our Anchor, Jesus's Anchor

In Mark's gospel, we read that when Jesus goes to the Garden of
Gethsemane, he falls to the ground and prays that, if possible,
the hour might pass from him. In his prayer, Jesus addresses
God as "Abba, Father" and, with complete faith, says, "Yet not
what I will, but what you will" (Mk 14:36). God the Father was
Jesus's anchor. When there was a threat to Jesus's own safety
and security, he fell to his knees in prayer and cried out to his
Father. In this poignant display of childlike trust, Jesus was
allowing himself to be parented by God.

I remember when I was in elementary school, I would play
outside with the neighbor kids. We would ride bikes or play
basketball, tag, or hide-and-seek without a care in the world.
One Saturday, we decided to play field hockey. We set up two
goals horizontally from one end of the sidewalk to the other
and began to play a game that none of us had played before.
Being the adventurous kid that I was (and still am), I was not
afraid to play with the boys and sprinted forward to steal the
puck from a kid much larger than myself. Suddenly I found
myself hurled several feet forward on the rough gravel, bleed-
ing profusely. I had never seen so much blood in my life.

In my agony, all I could think to do was cry out to my step dad, whom I call my dad, as I lay there badly bruised, scraped, and hurting. I did not care what the other kids thought or the high probability that I would never get to play field hockey again—all I wanted was my Abba. As I cried and cried, desperate for my dad to hear me from inside the house, he suddenly ran out the door, scooped me up in his arms, held me close, and brought me inside, where he tended to my wound. Looking back, I can identify that I intuitively knew I could not get anchored alone. I needed to allow myself to cry out.

At that moment in my own insecurity and unsafety, God was my anchor through the responsiveness and tenderness of my dad. My dad brought safety, security, and hope to my fearful heart. That is what we want to experience with our Father in heaven always. We want to have an assurance that when we cry out to him, when we are badly hurting and feeling wounded, he will come in to scoop us up and bring us close to him.

Reclaiming Our Anchor in God

For some of us, this might not be possible (yet). We may need to grow in our understanding of the Father and increase our feeling of safety and trust in God. This sense of safety and security with God can be achieved when we begin to process our experiences, especially our experiences with our family of origin and what we have been taught about God. It can also be possible when we learn how to connect with God in ways that can work toward reclaiming our anchor in God.

Throughout the rest of this chapter, we will have several opportunities to connect with God and our inner child through the practice of resourcing. Resourcing is an eye movement desensitization reprocessing (EMDR) technique that we can use to identify and instill coping skills to help us deal with difficult reactions that we may experience. We can use resourcing to move us out of feelings of mistrust and unsafety with God toward the possibility that God can be safe and expansive enough to care for whatever we are presented with.

As a result, we can experience more integration and better understand and rebuild trust with our inner child and God. We participate in the Father's divine parenting and, in God's restorative embrace, experience the love that heals us.

Ruah: God's Breath, Our Breath

One of the easiest ways to experience God's restorative embrace and reparent our inner child is through our breath. Our breath is powerful. It works with our parasympathetic nervous system to bring regulation to our entire body. It is also our lifeline that binds us back to God and back to our imago dei. In Hebrew, *breath* is called *ruah* or "breath of life," and it also happens to be the same word for "Spirit." We see this word, *ruah,* in Genesis: "The LORD God formed man of dust from the ground, and breathed into his nostrils the breath of life; and man became a living soul" (2:7). From Genesis, *ruah* continues to show up throughout scripture, and it reaches its culmination when Jesus gives his apostles and their successors the Holy Spirit: "'Peace be with you. As the Father has sent me, even so I send you.' And when he had said this, he breathed on them, and said to them, 'Receive the Holy Spirit'" (Jn 20:21–23). Jesus breathed on the apostles, just as God breathed into Adam.

It is the breath of God, the Holy Spirit alive in us, that makes us living and thriving beings capable of accomplishing what we have been commissioned to do. When we are in a state of dysregulation, hypoarousal, or hyperarousal, we are not living and thriving beings. We are surviving beings. We are barely functioning beings or, for some of us, even spiritually and emotionally dead beings. We are not truly alive, and if we are not truly alive, we cannot truly heal. Only living things are given the opportunity to heal.

That is why each time we take an intentional and deep breath and call on the name of the Holy Spirit, we remember we are the imago dei, and we step into our Spirit-led adult self and connect with our Creator. We do not remain in what is pulling us toward death. The Lord animates our entire self, including all of our parts.

Befriending Work: Intentional Breathing

There are many ways to practice intentional deep breathing, but the important thing is to remember that we must engage our core, bring the breath all the way up to our lungs and chest, and then slowly bring the breath back down to our belly. With each inhale, we can call on the name of the Holy Spirit, and then with each exhale, we can intentionally surrender to Jesus something that is burdening us. Let's try it now. Just take three intentional breaths. See if you can connect with your mind, body, and soul.

This way of breathing is a simple strategy to anchor ourselves quickly and allow God to animate us. We can use this tool throughout our day, especially when noticing our wounded child or protective part coming up.

The Gift of Our Senses

Engaging with our five senses is another great tool to anchor ourselves. God has created us with five wonderful senses that can help us get more in touch with our body and with him. Using our senses, we can look around and take in the present moment. We can fix our gaze on a comforting image or go outside and wonder at the beauty of nature. We can taste something that awakens us—drink some ice-cold water, sip on a hot cup of coffee, chew a minty piece of gum, or eat a delicious snack. We can smell something delightful—a fragrant candle, calming essential oils, or fresh flowers. We can tune our ears to the sounds of our environment or put on a soothing song. We can also wrap ourselves in a warm blanket, use sensory tools or stress balls, or engage in safe touch such as putting one hand on our heart and one hand on our belly or asking for a hug from a loved one. There are many ways we can use our senses to support our well-being and anchor ourselves in God.

Mental Safety

It can also be helpful to identify a safe word or phrase, a safe image, and a safe, calm place that we can go to in our mind's eye. If you have been participating in the inner child meditations, you are always invited to go to a safe, calm place. It does not matter if the place is real or imagined; the safe, calm place helps us to go to a space in our mind that brings us peace. I have clients who go to beautiful grand cathedrals, small ornate chapels, lakes, beaches, the top of mountains, luscious gardens, or a friend, relative, or grandparent's house or other places they enjoyed as a child. These places can bring safety and security to our bodies and help us to experience God's presence. We can even conjure up an image of God by inviting God the Father, Jesus, or the Holy Spirit to be with us there.

Our mind's eye is truly incredible and capable of supporting our healing when we keep our focus on these comforting images. Many therapy models rely on the power of images to enter into a dialogue with our unconscious mind and bring to light what has been shrouded in darkness. St. Ignatius of Loyola believed in the power of images and taught others to pray with them, which he referred to as "contemplation." When praying with images, St. Ignatius believed we could better notice what God was trying to communicate ("What Is Ignatian Spirituality?").

From a nervous system perspective, contemplation aids in our body's relaxation. When our bodies begin to relax, we can begin anchoring with intellectual truths. We can do this by coming up with safe and calming words that remind us of the gift of our belovedness and God's presence with us. For example, as God's children, we can confidently make the following statements as we hold on to the calming image in our minds:

- I am safe.

- I am held.

- I am free.

- I am loved.

- It is going to be okay.

We can also utter:

- The name of Jesus.

- Come, Holy Spirit.

- Jesus, I trust in you.

- Draw near to me, O Lord.

It can be helpful to repeat these truths over and over again and synchronize them with our deep breaths.

Befriending Work: Resting in the Truth

Let us take a moment to practice this tool now. Think of your safe, calm place, and try to fully enter the place using all of your senses. If you have been doing the meditations at the end of each chapter, you probably already have a place in mind, but it is okay if you receive an image of a new place. Trust that the Holy Spirit will give you the right image. Once you are in your place and taking in all of the sights, sounds, smells, tastes, and things you can touch, see if you can use a safe, calm word or phrase to anchor you in God further. Repeat the safe word or phrase several times until your body fully relaxes.

Rooted in Jesus's Sacred Heart

Another strategy we can practice to anchor ourselves in God is to imagine the Sacred Heart of Jesus. I love using this image because the Sacred Heart of Jesus is the symbol of love. It was popularized after St. Margaret Mary Alacoque received visions, beginning in 1673, of the Sacred Heart as an image of a heart on fire adorned by a crown of thorns. Jesus told St. Margaret Mary that the flames represented his love for humanity, and the thorns represented our sinfulness and ingratitude. Before St. Margaret Mary died in 1690, she received the last rites and said, "I need nothing but God, and to lose myself in the heart of Jesus" ("St. Margaret Mary Alacoque").

For St. Margaret Mary, God was her anchor, and he was with her until her dying breath. When we go through experiences that remove us from our imago dei, our body moves to self-protection, and our protective part will do what they have always done to keep us safe. Therefore, recalling God in these moments and using an image of Jesus, such as his Sacred Heart, can help us slow down and become grounded in Christ. Let us try sitting with the image now using a grounding exercise I created for my clients.

Befriending Work: Sacred Heart Grounding

Think of an image of Jesus's Sacred Heart. Imagine the image being really far from you, so far that it is barely visible. Then practice deep breathing, and with each breath, say, "Jesus, I trust in you." Using your breath, imagine bringing the image closer to you. Repeat several times until the image becomes so close that you "lose yourself in the heart of Jesus."

The Gift of the Left and Right Sides of Our Brains

Another way we can anchor ourselves is by bringing integration to the left and right sides of the brain. According to neuroscientist and psychologist Dr. Dan Siegel, our left brains love and desire order (Siegel and Bryson, 15). When we connect with our left brain, our Spirit-led adult self shines. We can experience rational thinking, linguistics, sequence, discernment, cause and effect, and so on. When we connect with our right brain, our child parts shine. We experience our social engagement system, where we can take in facial expressions, tone of voice, posture, and gestures to communicate that we are safe. We can also use our emotions and memories.

When we experience dysregulation, it is difficult to access the truth. Our left brains essentially go offline. Our right brain becomes overactive because it senses that we are no longer safe and secure. Therefore, we move away from our imago dei (ventral vagal state) and into either hypoarousal (dorsal state, where our wounded child usually becomes more activated) or hyperarousal (sympathetic state, where our protective part usually becomes more activated). We end up using only part of our brains rather than bringing our whole selves to the moment, which is why the integration of the left and right hemispheres of our brains is so important.

A tool to help with integrating the left and right sides of our brains is bilateral stimulation, an EMDR technique also called "resource tapping." When we use bilateral stimulation, we can support the left and right hemispheres to join forces to process traumatic memories better. For the purpose of anchoring, we can also use it to bring grounding in the present moment.

A method of bilateral stimulation that I find helpful is the butterfly hug. This technique was developed by Lucina Artigas while working with survivors of Hurricane Pauline in 1997. Let's take a moment to practice this technique now.

Befriending Work: The Butterfly Hug Exercise

- Cross your arms over your chest so that the tip of the middle finger from each hand is placed below the collarbone. Hands and fingers should be as vertical as possible so that the fingers point toward the neck, not the arms.

- Then close your eyes or gently gaze at something comfortable in the room (after you have read the instructions).

- Then alternate the movement of your hands like a butterfly flapping its wings. Do this as rhythmically as possible.

- Take deep belly breaths as you continue to focus on what is happening in your body.

- Continue this until your body feels calm, grounded, soft, light, or unburdened.

The Gift of Order, Structure, Rest, and Play

It is also important to create order, structure, and time for rest and play for our inner child. Remember, our inner child is a child. They need to know they are safe and secure, and a great way to build safety and security is by having daily structure. When there is no order and structure, our inner child can become dysregulated. They can start to feel anxious, bored, or frustrated and then try to rule over our adult self.

Having daily structure can help with that—for example, having a morning and night routine, having a prayer routine, and engaging in meaningful work (child-rearing, professional work, volunteering, and so on). It can also be helpful to have designated times to rest and play. For example, we can set up specific times to engage with our loved ones, play a board game, go out for a run, dance, create something, watch the sunset, read a book, and so on. This intentional planning will also help us to connect more intimately with our imago dei, who loves to play and rest!

When we designate time to create structure, order, rest, and play, we must remember not to get too rigid. There must be room for fluidity and spontaneity too. Many people describe living a very structured and ordered life in childhood, and yet they do not feel anchored. The structure was too rigid, making them feel suffocated, dominated, dissociated, or disconnected. Many people experience the other extreme; they have not experienced structure or order at all. They learned to go wherever the wind takes them; as a result, they often describe feeling lost, confused, dissociated, and disconnected. This is why structure and order must be balanced and include rest and play. Balance helps us to move from extremes. Like a boat anchored to the bottom of the water, we do not have to be rocked or tossed away by the heavy winds or raging waters. We can be steady and find our rhythm.

The Gift of Connection

When we are integrated, we feel safe and secure. We feel as if we can finally rest. Connection helps us to be in our ventral vagal state, where our imago dei shines. We are not afraid of resting in the arms of another, being our most authentic self in the presence of others, or sharing our truest feelings in a conversation. In order to experience connection in our adult lives and integration with our imago dei, however, we must permit ourselves to be vulnerable. In Dr. Brené Brown's *The Gifts of Imperfection*, she describes vulnerability as a healing and connecting agent: "Staying vulnerable is a risk we have to take if we want to experience connection" (Brown, 70). We have to open ourselves to the chance of rejection, misunderstanding, or even abandonment. If we want to stay anchored and not fight, flee, freeze, or even fawn our way through life, we must therefore reach out to others. We have to allow people to coregulate us. We will need to admit our imperfections and our need for another. We can do this by phoning a friend, asking someone safe to pray with us, or asking a friend to walk with us outside. Walking with a safe person can be very anchoring because it connects and targets our left and right brains (bilateral stimulation). It can also regulate our heart rate and support our cognitive functioning (it brings out our adult self).

We can also connect with our Holy Mother, guardian angel, and the saints. Specifically, Mary is someone we want to confidently turn to often because, through her motherly embrace, she can receive us and comfort us as only a mother can. St. Teresa of Calcutta would often call on our Holy Mother and say, "Mary, Mother of Jesus, please be a mother to me now" (Gardiner). We can use this prayer, too, throughout our day.

The reality is that sometimes we do not have a safe person to turn to or are still struggling to let God be our anchor. God understands. He wants us to experience the power of safe relationships, and we can trust that developing safe relationships with God's mother, holy men and women, our guardian angel, and those closest to us will help us develop an even stronger relationship with God.

Befriending Work: Connecting with Others

Take a moment to try to connect with others now. Call or text a safe person, and let them know you are thinking about them. Or, using imaginative prayer, imagine having a dialogue with a particular saint or our Holy Mother in your safe, calm place. Let them know what is coming up for you while reading this chapter. Notice how you feel.

Getting Anchored Takes Time

It is important to emphasize that anchoring can be a long and grueling process. Depending on how dysregulated we feel, we may need to practice several of these tools for several minutes, hours, and even days, and that is okay.

We do not want to rush through anchoring to reach the next step. Our inner child needs a regulated Spirit-led adult self and their true anchor, God. Therefore, we can stay in this step for as long as we need. If we try to rush through this process, we might try to fix our inner child quickly instead of compassionately drawing near to our child parts and their deeper needs. We also might respond reactively. Reactivity often happens when we are not anchored enough.

For example, we may notice that we are not doing well, and instead of anchoring, we might continue with our day. Then when we are with a friend, family member, partner, or spouse, we may respond very impatiently, critically, or even violently. We can do this with our inner child too.

We need our inner child to understand that their needs and feelings matter, but we won't be able to respond to them until we are anchored first. We must also remember that we do not need to achieve perfect trust and faith in God to do this healing work. Ultimately, healing is a grace. The Lord will continue to work within us and help us to experience what our inner child needs most. All we have to do is stay patient and keep practicing whatever resource or coping strategy works for us most.

Our inner child will also need our consistency, so we must do our best to keep using the resources, even when we may not feel like it or don't seem to achieve the desired results. When we struggle to get anchored or simply do not feel like doing the slow and uncomfortable work it sometimes takes, we must remember to use what is easiest to do first, which typically is a deep breath, and then move to more complex strategies.

Lord, Save Me!

In the end our goal is to look a lot like Peter, who also found himself among treacherous winds and waves. In Matthew's gospel, we read that Peter sees Jesus walking on the turbulent water and confidently proclaims, "Bid me come to you on the water." In Peter's distress, he wants to walk toward Christ, not away from him. Jesus, knowing this, tells Peter, "Come." At that moment, Peter places his faith in Jesus, then gets out of the boat and walks on the water toward him. His eyes are fixed on his anchor.

However, in Peter's humanness, he begins to look around at the heavy winds and starts to become afraid, and he eventually sinks. But Peter does not stay there below the water. He recognizes his need for God. He doesn't lose the truth that he still has his anchor, and he cries out, "Lord, save me!" Immediately Jesus reaches out his hand and brings him up above the water, and Peter is saved (Mt 15:22–33).

As we apply this scripture passage to our healing work, we admit that our journey forward is not about never sinking or becoming so anchored that we become entirely still and fixated on Jesus. We will sink sometimes. We will feel overwhelmed by our inner child and focus on all the chaos around us or even within us. It is a part of being human, but the power of our anchor is that even when this happens, we have something and someone inside us that won't allow us to drown. When we cry out and keep using the tools that help us to connect with God, we will restore our safety and security. We will be anchored and have the capacity to rise above the water and befriend our inner child again.

Prayer

Father, thank you for being my anchor. My hope and my healing are in you. Deepen my trust in you. Help me slow down, use the tools I am learning, and reach out my hand to hold you, trusting you will hold me. Amen.

7

Acknowledge

We come to know our inner child well by becoming well acquainted with our body. Our body is a sacred gift, revealing hidden treasures about who we really are and what we really hold inside. In the words of St. John Paul II, "Science can examine our flesh in minute detail, down to our cells and even our DNA. But no amount of scientific exploration can replace the truth that our bodies reveal to us, giving form to our innermost being and unique personality. . . . Our bodies are sacramental—they make the invisible visible"(John Paul II 2009, 13).

Our inner child is one of those invisible realities that we hold within us, and our body can make the child within us visible. For example, somatic symptoms can point to how our inner child feels, and different illnesses can point to the trauma our inner child holds. Unfortunately, we live in a world that does not prioritize and dignify our bodies. Instead, a lot of messages have taught us to ignore, hate, degrade, or be indifferent toward our bodies.

In order to develop a healthy relationship with our body and, as a result, our inner child, we must carefully examine our view of our body and where this perspective comes from. When we have a mindset that does not respect and honor our body, we will carry that in our approach to inner child work.

St. Paul wrote in his First Letter to the Corinthians, "Do you not know that you are God's temple and that God's Spirit dwells in you?" (3:16). When we care for our body well by eating nutritious foods, sleeping enough, exercising regularly, setting boundaries that protect our body, and practicing temperance, modesty, chastity, obedience, and self-advocacy, our inner child can begin to heal because we are treating the temple that they reside in with respect and care. So, when we bathe, feed, defend, nourish, and support our body, our inner child receives the message that they are worthy of respect and care. However, when we are not good stewards over our body, our inner child can start to feel ashamed, guilty, worthless, and even disgusted with their own self. They essentially receive the message that they are not worth loving.

Juan's Story

Juan had used food to cope for many years. He had learned very early in childhood that his wounded child would calm down when he was eating unhealthy foods. When he was eating these foods, he wouldn't sense his ache for connection, acceptance, and nurture. It was as if his wounded child was finally happy.

Now at fifty-three years old, when he came to therapy, he had so much repressed anger, frustration, disappointment, and sadness. He was trying to lose weight, but he had no idea what to do with the feelings that came up when he was no longer eating what he wanted. In an effort to protect himself further, therefore, he began using other unhealthy ways to cope that only degraded his body even more.

Juan's body became the punching bag that stored all of his unhealed wounds and harmful childhood experiences. Self-harm, daily masturbation, pushing his body to unhealthy limits through highly intense workouts, and even skin-picking became additional punches that left him feeling bruised and badly beaten. Needless to say, Juan did not feel like his body was a temple. Juan hated his body, or so he thought. As we unpacked his story, we learned that Juan really hated the fragmenting four that his inner child had suffered.

Unfortunately, Juan was a victim of sexual abuse by the age of seven, was exposed to porn by the age of ten, started to self-harm by the age of twelve, and witnessed the long demise of his parents' marriage throughout his entire childhood until the age of eighteen, when he finally moved out. Juan's body was not celebrated or protected, so he could not see that there was something inside of him worth celebrating and protecting either.

When I learned more about Juan and his story, I knew I would need to help Juan develop the proper reverence and respect for his body before we started acknowledging his inner child. So we started to become more aware of how he was feeling in his body. We used a simple tool called a body scan, which can be especially helpful in inner child work.

Befriending Work: The Body Scan

Just take a few moments to disengage from the contents of this book and become aware of how your body feels right now. Use your breath to help slow you down and tune out any noise around you.

- Begin with the top of your head and then move down to your face, and see if you can notice any sensations.

- Then draw your attention to your chest, heart region, shoulders, upper back, and throat. See if you can notice anything within this region.

- Now move your awareness down to your lower back, abdominal, and pelvic area.

- Then shift your attention to your upper thighs, glutes, shins, and calves.

- Lastly, move your awareness to your ankles, feet, and toes.

- Take a moment to reflect in your journal on what you noticed, and see if you can connect any specific sensation to a child part.

Juan's Inner Child Work

Our inner child constantly communicates important truths through sensations in our bodies. Interestingly, our protective part will show up most in our chest and shoulder region as a feeling of tightness or restriction. It is as if it is communicating, "I am carrying the weight of the world to protect you!" Certainly, in Juan's case, this proved to be true. Juan had been under a tremendous amount of pressure all of his life. Juan always felt responsible for his parents' marriage, and it carried into his own marriage: Juan felt overly responsible for his wife's happiness and for being the best father he could be. He was putting too much pressure on himself never to show his wounded child or his protective part and to keep it all together. When his fractured parts would inevitably find their way to the surface, he would punish himself. Despite Juan's best efforts not to be like his parents, he found himself repeating the same harmful behaviors, and as a result, his marriage suffered.

As we unraveled all the different layers in his story, we continued to acknowledge his body and would notice when his body would shift and change, and each time we noticed the shift, we would talk about it. As we acknowledged his body, we started to notice a pattern. Juan would show up with pressure and tension, and then at the end of the session, he would leave feeling relaxed and open.

Juan was acknowledging his inner child by simply tuning in to the sensations in his body and, as a result, the pressure and tension in his body would lift. He allowed himself to become aware of what he was feeling without harsh judgment or quick fixes. Juan was more compassionate toward himself. Juan could see that every time he neglected his body, was harsh, restricting, or punishing toward his body, he was inflicting suffering on his inner child, and he slowly began to stop.

We are invited to this same compassion. We can acknowledge our inner child by first acknowledging and taking care of our body. The more we take care of our body, the easier it will be to understand when our inner child is in need of our care and to show up for our inner child with reverence and respect.

Acknowledgment Heals

So many of us underestimate how much acknowledgment heals us. When I was in graduate school, we were often told that it did not truly matter which psychological theory we ascribe to or how we choose to practice therapy. All that matters is our presence and the way we acknowledge our clients' feelings. I see this all the time in my work. When I develop a strong rapport with clients and acknowledge their feelings well, they leave each session feeling seen, heard, and known. They feel safe and secure, ready to tackle whatever challenge they are presented with.

Many of us have experienced a lack of acknowledgment in childhood because, unfortunately, the adults who were entrusted to care for us were not anchored enough to see our pain, hear our cries, and know us deeply. Only a person who is truly anchored can move toward the winds and waves without being swept away by the chaos, as we read in the last chapter, which is what we see with Jesus. Jesus is so united with God that he can always acknowledge what is broken and in need of love and healing without it stealing his equilibrium and peace.

We see this in the scripture story of the woman who bled for twelve years. Jesus is walking and is pressed upon by a large crowd of people, but he feels a woman touch the fringe of his garment. Jesus suddenly stops what he is doing and asks, "Who was it that touched me?" Jesus could have kept going. He could have ignored the feeling, but instead, he acknowledges that a wounded woman has touched him. Jesus does this because he knows the woman needs him and because of her own acknowledgment of her woundedness. Jesus tells her, "Daughter, your faith has made you well; go in peace" (Lk 8:42–48).

With Eyes Wide Open

On my own healing journey with inner child work, I frequently could not acknowledge my inner child because it did steal my equilibrium. I was far from being anchored in God. My inner child revealed to me an entire galaxy of hard truths: painful connections between the past and present, generational ties that went way deeper than mere coincidence, suppressed feelings from my earliest years of life, and a plethora of unspoken thoughts that relayed my innermost beliefs, and with the truth came grief, disgust, anger, frustration, and sorrow, all feelings I didn't want to feel. Sometimes, all I wanted to do was go back to a life of sin because at least I did not have to feel the pain as much.

I share this in a spirit of accompaniment. As you read through part 1 of this book, you may have already felt deeply troubled or scared by what you have started to acknowledge within yourself. We must remember that this work will not be easy, especially if we have learned to disconnect from our body, emotions, or parts of our inner child, but it is transformative and necessary work. Without it, we cannot be our real selves. We will have wasted our one precious life living a lie. When our inner child "touches" us, they are being honest. They are telling us something that we need to hear. They are showing us something that we need to see. It will always be challenging to slow down and become aware, stop walking toward wherever we are headed, and ask, "Who touched me?" But when we do, everything changes, and we experience healing.

The Language of Acknowledgment

When we acknowledge our inner child, we are learning how to connect our bodily feelings and emotions to a specific part of our inner child. For example, after we have identified that we have a significant amount of chest pain, we can connect that with a specific emotion. We might notice through our body's cues that we are experiencing fear. We then can connect that emotion to our wounded child since our wounded child carries our more raw and vulnerable feelings.

All of our emotions will connect with a specific part of our inner child. Consider reviewing your befriending work from part 1 to remember what each part of you holds.

Befriending Work: Acknowledging the Parts

Now, take a moment to construct a table like the one below, including what each part typically feels and where you feel it in your body.

	Imago Dei	Wounded Child	Protective Part	Adult Self
Characteristics	Reflects the image and likeness of God. The imago dei is our authentic core.	Reflects our core wounds, painful emotions, and core beliefs that have fractured us from our imago dei.	Reflects our defense mechanisms, pride, anger, control, and mistrust.	Reflects our rational thinking and will, as well as the gifts and the fruits of the Holy Spirit.
States	Often in a state of social engagement: pure, free, creative, open-minded, trusting, spirited, present, imaginative, playful, connected, and full of wonder, awe, and delight. Also reflects our individual strengths and temperament.	Often in a state of hypoarousal: withdrawal, passivity, disconnection, hopelessness, emptiness, shutdown.	Often in a state of hyperarousal: anxiety, obsessive thinking, defensiveness, tension, hypervigilance, reactivity.	Often in a state of regulation: awareness, presence, safety, compassion, curiosity, leadership and agency.
Functions	Helps us to see God alive in us and to use our God-given strengths to share our God-given light.	Internalizes harmful experiences and communicates our deepest hurts and unmet needs.	Protects our wounded child from experiencing the same wounds.	Brings integration and the gifts of the Holy Spirit to our internal fracture so that our inner child can receive God's healing and reparenting.
Feelings/ Emotions	Joyful, rested, giddy, energized, peaceful, receptive, etc.	Sad, anxious, scared, restless, insecure, longing, powerless, and lonely.	Angry (covert and overt expressions), impatient, fearful, heavily burdened.	Empowered, strong, resilient, hopeful, courageous, compassionate, calm, curious, connected, etc.
Bodily Sensations	Openness, warmth, softness, ease, etc.	Discomfort, nausea, tearfulness, tingling, cold/ shivery, etc.	Tightness, pressure, headache, hot, fidgety, etc.	Energized, alive, awake, expanded, releasing, etc.

It is possible that all of your parts may feel happy, energized, calm, or peaceful. That's okay. The point is not only to identify distress but to become more aware of our body and emotional state. After identifying the emotional and physical feelings and the child part each is connected to, we can start acknowledging our child parts in real time. When we notice our wounded child or protective part, we can say something mentally, such as the following:

- "I see your suffering."

- "I see how sad you are."

- "I feel how much you are carrying."

- "I am sensing you are really anxious."

- "I know you are angry."

- "I understand how triggered you are right now."

- "I am a little busy right now, but I hear you. I will check in with you later."

Acknowledging, Not Changing

Oftentimes, when we begin acknowledging our inner child, we may wish to fix our distressing feelings or say something positive to help release them. Inner child work is indeed empowering work, and yet, we must be careful not to rush to change our feelings. In fact, sitting with our inner child's feelings can be more empowering than trying to "fix" the feelings, because when we do, we offer self-compassion. We are making space for what might have been previously silenced, rejected, bypassed, or shamed, and we are naming those feelings—for some of us, it is for the first time. We also give our inner child an opportunity to experience new feelings—more positive feelings over time. We address an unmet need since many of us were not taught the language of our emotions or were not seen, heard, known, or pursued in our emotional distress in childhood.

So often we underestimate the power of showing up in this way with ourselves and with others. But if you have a child in your life, or the next time a friend, family member, spouse, or colleague has a big emotion, try to acknowledge their feelings in a loving and compassionate tone. Again, do not try to fix or offer a solution. Just point out what you are observing, and see what happens. When I practice this, I typically notice the following:

- Bodies relaxing

- Defensive walls lowering

- Openness and receptivity

- An increase in communication

- Connection

Acknowledgment truly heals us. We are allowing ourselves to be seen, heard, and known, and as we do, we challenge unhealthy messages such as these that have kept us hiding, afraid, and interiorly divided:

- "Put on a brave face."

- "You just have to choose to be happy."

- "Think of people who have it worse."

- "Think of how much worse the generations before you had it."

- "It's just life."

- "It's just your period."

- "It's just depression, anxiety, or another psychological disorder."

- "Just offer it up."

- "Just pray more."

As we challenge these demeaning and oversimplified messages and draw near to our inner child in a way that honors them, we get to the heart of what we are actually experiencing, and as a result, we become more whole. We become more connected to our child parts and give them a fighting chance to live out their dignity and worth and to embrace new messages:

- "We don't always have to put on a happy face."
- "It is brave to confront our feelings."
- "We can be curious about our emotions instead of judgmental."
- "We can honor the challenges in the generations that came before and honor our own unique challenges."
- "Pain and suffering are inevitable, and yet, we can still have a beautiful life."
- "Our physical ailments and hormonal changes can unearth hidden things we bury; we can move from what is at face value and take a closer look."
- "Our symptoms may be a part of a psychological disorder we are struggling with, but it doesn't fully communicate the complexity of who we are."
- "We can offer up what we experience and explore what we experience."
- "We can pray daily about our experiences, and we may still need psychological support, guidance, and additional resources."

Prayer

Father, I hear the cry of my inner child. I am beginning to feel and understand my inner child better and how they show up in my body. Help me to see that my inner child's needs and feelings are valid. Help me to care for my body better. Help me to acknowledge my inner child as you do, especially when life is challenging and overwhelming. Amen.

8

Attune

"I am worried that I won't be able to connect to my inner child," Lily fretted. "I am just not very maternal."

"I understand, Lily. It makes sense that you would feel that way given your experiences with your own mother," I responded.

Lily nodded and then inquired, "So, what do I do?"

"We practice," I said. "We have to practice attuning to your inner child. It won't be easy, but I know you have it in you."

How did I know that Lily had it in her? Well, because as we acknowledge our inner child, it becomes more and more natural to attune to our inner child. Through attunement, we can respond to our inner child's needs and emotions and draw into their suffering. As we grow in knowledge and understanding, we develop empathy for our inner child. Once we have identified our inner child parts, their wounds, story, internalized beliefs, distressing feelings, self-protections, vows and agreements, and how they show up in our bodies, we cannot help but draw near to these parts of ourselves.

The Importance of Attunement

Attunement is one of the most emotionally intimate displays of affection, and being on the receiving end of it touches on our heart's deepest desires. From the moment we took our first breath, we have been on a quest for validation, intimacy, affection, love—everything that attunement provides. Without someone to attune to us, we will always struggle to know whether or not we are known, seen, heard, or loved. We will even struggle to know who we are, and over time, we will be severed from what we yearn for most—love.

Attunement during the first three years of life helped set the foundation for our attachment style. Many of our needs were met if our mother was highly attuned to us. If our mother was highly attuned, we were given milk when we cried. When we were scared, we were rocked and held until we calmed down. When we had a bowel movement, we were cleaned and dried. If this was our experience, during these highly stressful times, we formed an association that our distressing feelings (emotionally and somatically) can be met with safety, comfort, and love.

However, for those of us like Lily who did not experience a highly attuned mother and have associated intense emotion with rejection, loneliness, absence, dismissiveness, annoyance, or apathy, we may struggle with attunement and feel very insecure within this step of the work, no matter how natural attunement is and how much we yearn for it.

Those of us with insecure attachment styles will struggle with attunement most because we do not have a secure relationship with ourselves or others. Emotional intimacy feels unsafe. We feel scared, ambivalent, or alarmed by the attention and care that attunement offers. We might even feel uncomfortable with the soft language or tenderness in an attuned response. Or we might find ourselves rejecting it or hearing a part of us that does not want to be seen, heard, known, or loved. We simply are not used to it.

Kenny's Story

Kenny, a client of mine, struggled with attunement with his wife and children, and like Lily, he was afraid that he would not be able to complete this step with his inner child. He and Lily had very different childhood experiences with their mothers. Lily grew up with an emotionally abusive mother who struggled with mental illness and addiction. She was dismissive and preoccupied and would often shut herself in her room for hours when she was having a depressive episode. Kenny, however, grew up with a kind and generous mother. He received a lot of affection through home-cooked meals and warm hugs, but Kenny's mother was never attuned to his emotions. She never asked him how he felt about anything. He was often encouraged to "be a good little boy" and obey.

Now let's look at how these two different upbringings form similar child parts. Lily and Kenny each have an easygoing imago dei who loves to make others happy, but their imago dei could not take root. Both Lily and Kenny's strengths were exploited, which caused an internal fracture that looked like a wounded child who is confused ("I don't understand why I am doing all the right things but still don't feel loved") and ashamed ("I must not be good enough for love. There must be something deeply wrong with me"). Naturally, the protective part used what they already had and offered up their imago dei's strengths for survival.

So when Lily and Kenny would look at themselves as adults, all they could see was a smiley and head-nodding people pleaser who felt emotionally dead inside. They lived with several inner vows such as "We cannot stand out; we have to blend in to be good enough," "We cannot have our own thoughts and opinions; we must assimilate and believe what the majority is thinking," and "We cannot share any real feelings so we can win the approval of others." With a protective part in leadership, an imago dei who was lost, and a Spirit-led adult self who was aware but had no idea how to effect change, it was clear why they were both apprehensive to attune.

Fortunately, Lily and Kenny and all of us like them are not bound to our childhood experiences. We can become more emotional, nurturing, and attuned individuals simply because we are made in the image and likeness of God, and God is highly attuned to us.

The God Who Attunes

Throughout scripture, we read how God attunes to us. God moves from mere acknowledgment to truly allowing himself to feel our emotions and respond to us emotionally. We read in Isaiah that the Lord is a "man of sorrows, and acquainted with grief" (53:3). When we are sad and hurting, Jesus weeps (see John 11:35). Jesus also responds to us with joy: "These things I have spoken to you, that my joy may be in you, and that your joy may be full" (Jn 15:11).

Imagine if Jesus just acknowledged us. His sadness, grief, and joy wouldn't be present, and he would be more distant and reserved toward us. He might even be indifferent. Jesus might say something like, "I see that you are blind," "I hear that you want me to heal you," "I can understand that you are like a sheep without a shepherd," but that would be it. Nothing else. Jesus would see us, but he wouldn't allow himself to feel us.

When we attune, we are practicing empathy. We are modeling our lives after Jesus and lovingly entering suffering. We are not just simply naming feelings and experiences but are allowing ourselves to be in communion with those feelings and experiences. We are practicing deep compassion.

Meeting Kinesha

During my senior year of undergrad, I co-led a trip of pilgrims to Kingston, Jamaica. I had the privilege of working alongside the Missionaries of Charity, St. Teresa of Calcutta's religious order, for a day. The Missionaries of Charity had a home that took in men and women whom the local community could not support.

During my day there, I encountered a woman whom my co-leader, Maddie, had described to me and told me about the night before.

"Kinesha?" I asked the woman.

With a coy grin, she nodded her head.

"Hi, I am Brya, Maddie's friend."

She politely smiled and then looked down.

"Would it be alright if I sat next to you?"

Kinesha nodded her head yes again and then looked away.

I admit, it was hard for me to look at her too. I wanted to look away. Kinesha had been suffering from HIV for the past couple of years, and her body was deteriorating. She was extremely frail. Her bones protruded through her skin, and every inch of her beautiful brown skin was discolored with a rash.

"Kinesha, I would love to learn more about you. How do you like it here?"

By acknowledging Kinesha and being curious about her experiences, I offered Kinesha an opportunity to be seen, heard, and known, which allowed her to share openly about her past and present. As I listened to Kinesha, my heart was moved. I found myself, little by little, drawing closer to her.

We were quickly moving from strangers to companions. Within a couple of hours, I learned so much about her. We discussed everything from her life before HIV to her love for beauty products and painting her nails.

I then asked, "Kinesha, since you really like painting your nails, would it be okay if I used that paint you have over there and painted your nails?"

Kinesha's eyes widened. "You are not allowed to touch me. Trust me, you wouldn't want to touch me," she fretted.

Kinesha was right. I was not allowed to touch her. Since Kinesha had HIV, we were told to wear gloves so we did not somehow contract the virus. Although I did not have the language for it back then, I could see now that Kinesha's protective part had entered the scene. Kinesha was most likely feeling my compassion, but it scared her. She was used to being cast aside and neglected by others, so to receive such an intimate request was probably foreign to her.

But I didn't care. I looked past her resistance and the rules, and without even realizing what I was doing, I picked up the nail polish she had, grabbed her frail hand, and began painting her nails. Kinesha smiled, and we continued to talk as if we had been friends for many years.

After her little nail beds were dazzled in pink, I gently blew on them to dry them and then helped her get ready for bed. As Kinesha lay in bed, now in her nightgown, we prayed the Rosary together before my departure.

Every word, every fingertip on each bead, every proclamation of a Hail Mary and an Our Father felt intentional. The prayers of our faith felt like a declaration of my hopes for Kinesha. I was feeling her pain and entrusting her to God, knowing that he felt what I was feeling too.

When it was time to leave, the pain in my chest felt unbearable, a pain I now feel as I write this.

"I wish I didn't have to leave you, Kinesha. I enjoyed my day with you. I am really going to miss you." Tears quietly rolled down my cheeks with each word of goodbye.

Kinesha's eyes filled with tears too. "Pray for me," she said.

"Yes, Kinesha. I will never forget you. I hope to see you one day in heaven."

Kinesha nodded, wiping the tears from the corners of her eyes, and then exclaimed, "Yes, me too!"

This encounter with a stranger is what it looks like when we allow ourselves to attune to another. Through the sharing of our hearts, we moved from mere acknowledgment to palpable connection, and because of that, we became united as one.

The Language of Attunement

When we attune to our inner child, we will have the opportunity to no longer be strangers but unified, just as in the experience between Kinesha and me. When Kinesha and I were tearful at the end, we mirrored each other. Kinesha allowed herself to be received, and I allowed myself to show up compassionately and then be received too. Through this exchange, our bodies began to synchronize like a mother and her baby. In other words, our mirror neurons were activated.

According to researchers, mirror neurons are seen as the biological basis of compassion. When we are highly attuned to one another and are compassionate, mirror neurons are firing. Our brains take each other's emotional responses and bring harmony. The sounds, tone, prosody, body posture, and facial gestures of others give us the cue to relax and connect and mirror their body language, affect, and tone.

We can apply this idea to our befriending of our inner child and help our inner child know they are safe to connect by the way we attune to them. We can be soft in our speech, mental tone, and bodies through anchoring. We can allow ourselves to see our fractured child parts and feel them. We can bring ourselves more deeply into their emotional states and reflect them back. We can also use words of compassion and validation. We can say phrases such as the ones in the list below.

- "I am so sorry you are going through this right now."
- "What you are experiencing is so painful."
- "It breaks my heart to see you so sad."
- "I am right here . . . I am right here . . ."
- "I can feel how worried you are."
- "Your anxiety is warranted."
- "Your anger makes sense!"
- "It is okay to feel upset right now."
- "Your feelings are valid."
- "Go ahead. You can cry. It's okay to cry."
- "Everyone gets scared sometimes trying something new. That's okay."
- "I am with you. I am not going anywhere."

So many of us are not used to responding to our emotional state in this way, but phrases such as these increase safety and security between our Spirit-led adult self and our inner child. They strengthen the bond of connection and bring cohesion and synergy. We need responses like these to experience healing.

Befriending Work: Speaking Words of Love

Take a moment now to reflect on what phrases your inner child may need to hear. What words of compassion and validation would best attune to their experience? Write them down in your journal.

Making Sense of Our Feelings

The more we attune to our inner child, the more we begin making sense of their feelings because we are allowing our inner child to be known intimately. For example, let's expand on some compassionate phrases we just examined:

- "Your anger makes sense! For so long, you have felt as if you were not allowed to be angry, but what was done to you was not okay. You have every reason to feel angry right now."

- "What you are experiencing is so painful. You want to be loved so badly, and you keep getting disappointed by the people you were hoping you could put your trust in."

- "It breaks my heart to see you so sad. I know the experiences we face right now probably feel like our experiences with Mom and Dad."

Our Spirit-led adult self can see the bigger reality. They can attune to the feelings of our inner child and also use our child self's experiences to make connections so our child self can feel understood.

Now let's practice this together through bilateral journaling. Remember the butterfly hug we practiced? We can use the exact same brain science to connect the left and right hemispheres of our brain and help our inner child make sense of their experiences through bilateral journaling.

Befriending Work: Bilateral Journaling

Bilateral journaling is a journaling technique I discovered that combines bilateral stimulation and inner child dialoguing. We begin by splitting our paper in half or drawing a line in the middle. We label the left side "adult self" and the right side "inner child." When dialoguing with our inner child, we begin with our dominant hand with the adult self on the left side and then move to our nondominant hand when we allow our child self to respond on the right side. Shifting from our dominant hand to our nondominant hand and from the left and right sides of the paper can help us integrate our left and right hemispheres as we did with the butterfly tapping. However, we do not have to, and we can still experience powerful results by using our dominant hand on both sides. The important thing is just to make sure we are shifting from the left and right side of our paper.

We start the dialogue by first acknowledging our inner child. We might say something like, "I see you are sad," "I am noticing your irritation," or "I can tell you miss Mom again." We may also not really know what our inner child is experiencing and will need to acknowledge by simply asking, "How are you feeling?"

After we ask our inner child a question or acknowledge what we noticed, we then wait to hear a response within us. Perhaps we may hear a thought like, "Yeah, I am so sad!" or "Yes! I am mad! Nobody ever pays attention to me!" We then write it down. Our job is to stay present and listen to the language of our hearts without trying to fix, change, or manipulate the conversation. We have to remain vulnerable and open and write down exactly what we hear in response to give our inner child the opportunity to be attuned well.

After we acknowledge our inner child and write down our inner child's response, we can then attune to the child. We might say, "I am so sorry; your sadness makes sense," or "Yeah, the anger is valid. Today was tough when our sister seemed to ignore what we had to say."

Attuning to Our Inner Child

This exercise may seem really strange, and I would be lying if I said it wasn't. We are dialoguing with ourselves, and we will see penmanship that will look like a child stole our paper and started writing for us. But we must stay with it. As we continue this practice of acknowledging and attuning, we will understand our inner child better, and as a result, we will feel more peace and have more clarity.

I can't tell you how many times I introduced this exercise to a client, and they looked at me somewhat puzzled yet intrigued. And then once they practiced it, they experienced life-changing results.

It is also possible that, when doing this exercise, we may feel uncomfortable with what we are hearing. Sometimes when we give our inner child space to respond back to us and to be heard, we may hear something that we have never been conscious of, or something that alarms, surprises, or even calls us out. We must lean into our discomfort and allow the Holy Spirit to keep us anchored as we make space for the feelings.

We also must stay patient. It will be challenging at first, especially if you choose to switch from your dominant hand to your nondominant hand, and it will be challenging if you struggle to hear anything from your inner child after you acknowledge them. However, our persistence and practice become the catalysts for our inner child to finally be heard and truly seen. Remember the images of your child self that came up in part 1. That child needs you to not give up on them. That child needs your practice, even when it is hard.

We may notice that when we try to do this exercise on our own, we want to work through the feelings and find a solution quickly. Perhaps it feels challenging to attune and stay in the hurt. We may find ourselves wanting to alleviate our inner child's distressing emotions. But attunement is the practice of compassionate presence. We are helping our child parts feel felt. That's it. We can trust, however, that we won't stay in the distressing emotions. There will be an interior movement that brings us closer to all that we long for simply because our inner child will feel loved.

Validating the Feelings, Not the Behavior

Some of us may still feel unsure about this step because we do not want to validate something wrong, impious, or sinful. We must remember that attunement is not excusing harmful behavior in ourselves or others. Instead, it is about connecting with the deeper emotional reality embedded in the behavior. We can still hold ourselves and others accountable for negative and sinful actions.

We might also feel wary of attuning to our inner child when we make a mistake or hurt someone with our actions or words. We might feel that we deserve to sit in shame, but these moments of imperfection are when our inner child needs us the most. When our inner child is partly responsible for our poor choices, we need to practice not vilifying or condemning ourselves but responding with care and concern to the feelings that led to the choice.

For example, many mothers might make a parenting mistake and immediately think, "I am such a bad mom! I cannot believe I can be so stupid! What is wrong with me?" Then they stay in those thoughts until the feelings become less intense or, perhaps, just trickle back down in their subconscious. But in this work, we acknowledge the shame and fear embedded in those thoughts, connect them to our child parts, and then attune to the emotions. In the next step, we will have an opportunity to support the behavior and meet our inner child's needs, but for now, we must remember that it is okay just to feel. It is okay to unearth hidden emotions, and it is okay to validate those emotions.

Our inner child is a child who longs to be attuned to and needs attunement to be a complete and whole self. So let us not get distracted by all the other noise, the "shoulds" and "should-nots." The self-judgments and echoes of the past told us that attunement is unnecessary or pitiful, but the truth is, we crave and need attunement.

At some point in our lives, we all have known what it is like to be attuned to—to have someone mirror our distressing feelings and extend Christ's compassion. Perhaps you are thinking of that person now who has given you a real example of what attunement looks like. Take a moment now just to reflect on how that impacted you. Perhaps you felt a lightness. A budding hope. A glimmer of joy. A spark of connection.

We must remember this as we engage in this step in the process. We want our inner child to experience these feelings whenever they call for us and need our attention and care. We want them to know they are worth hearing, seeing, knowing, and feeling. They are worth all it takes to live as God's beloved child again.

Prayer

Father, I feel the emotions of my inner child. Like a mother and her newborn baby, help me to respond to these emotions with nurture. Give me the grace to attune to my inner child just as you attune to me. Amen.

9

Ask

We read in Luke's gospel that while Jesus is traveling to Jerusalem near Jericho, a man named Bartimaeus, who was born blind, calls out to him from the roadside. Bartimaeus, desperate to be healed by Jesus, shouts above the crowd that came to see Jesus, "Son of David, have mercy on me!" Those around him hush him, but he shouts even louder, "Son of David, have mercy on me!" Jesus, hearing his cries, responds to Bartimaeus with a question, "What do you want me to do for you?" Bartimaeus then utters what he desires most: "Lord, let me receive my sight" (Lk 18:35–43).

Our inner child is a lot like Bartimaeus. Our inner child wants to see their worth, value, and whether they are safe and loved. They shout above all the other noises in our life, desperate to receive these answers. After we acknowledge and attune to our inner child, we uncover what their deepest desires are. We do this by asking the question that Jesus asked Bartimaeus: "What do you want me to do for you?"

Safe to Ask and Not Assume

Growing up, when adults asked about our emotional world, it helped us meet our needs. It increased our security and our sense of being loved. If we did not experience this, we learned that what we need and feel does not really matter. We also learned that inquiry and leading with curiosity are not very important, and as a result, we make many assumptions instead, such as these:

133

- "I am just having a bad day."
- "They probably are just tired."
- "I am sure I am just overworked."
- "That person is a jerk!"
- "People don't really care."

Most of our assumptions come from what we hear in childhood. As children, we were taught what to think and even how to think or not to think. We often were limited in exploring our curiosity. Around three or four, when our brains were forming more complex thoughts and were full of wonder, many of our questions were met with annoyance or nonanswers. We might also have felt silenced or shamed when we asked questions. When this is our early childhood experience, we will struggle to use our voice, which prevents us from asking the right questions to get our needs met and even to support and care for others.

Our protective part may also use assumptions to calm our wounded child's fears, uncertainty, doubt, insecurity, or anxiety. This part of us constantly responds to the patterns or mental models we take from our environment to make meaning of what we experience. But making assumptions blocks us from God's healing work and prevents us from giving and receiving love. We generalize and minimize a person or our own experience when we assume. Assumptions leave little room for the truth. Therefore, we must use our curiosity to start asking questions and also communicate to our inner child that it is safe to be heard. It is the only way we can get their needs met.

In dysfunctional families, we are often taught that we have to figure things out ourselves and suppress our needs. Asking for help is synonymous with being weak, lazy, or dependent, and communicating our needs is often synonymous with self-ishness. In this work, however, we need to gain comfort with asking questions and being heard because, as we see with Jesus and Bartimaeus, it is the way we receive healing.

Reaching the Heart

When Jesus asks questions in the gospels, he always gets to the heart of the matter:

- "Who do you say that I am?" (Mt 16:15).
- "Do you want to be healed?" (Jn 5:6).
- "Do you now believe?" (Jn 16:31).
- "Why did you doubt?" (Mt 14:31).
- "Do you love me?" (Jn 21:17).
- "Why are you troubled, and why do questionings rise in your hearts?" (Lk 24:38).
- "What do you want me to do for you?" (Mk 10:51).
- "Why are you weeping? Whom do you seek?" (Jn 20:15).
- "Why do you call me 'Lord, Lord,' and not do what I tell you?" (Lk 6:46).

Therefore, asking our inner child a question is meant to reach their heart. We might ask questions like the following:

- How are you feeling?
- What's going on for you right now?
- What do you need from me?
- Can you help me understand why you think or feel like that?
- Did something trigger you recently?
- Why are you afraid?

Specifically for the protective part, we might ask:

- What would you need to believe? To feel safe? To surrender? To trust?
- Why do you feel you need to protect me in this way?
- What's making you feel so angry?

When I started inner child work, I was afraid to ask my inner child questions. My adult self and protective part had all kinds of judgments about this work. I began to wonder, *If I engage in this work, does that mean I have multiple personality disorder or dissociative identity disorder?* I feared that I would feel crazier than I already felt. I was used to asking questions as a therapist, with friends, and even with family members, but it felt foreign to ask myself questions. But then, each time I tried it, I received a response. It was not something auditory but rather a thought that would come up fairly quickly that seemed connected to a child part.

If it were not for my inquiry, I would not have learned that often when I am feeling off, my inner child wants to play and connect. Or when I am feeling frustrated, my inner child wants to feel seen and heard. Or when I am feeling sad, my inner child needs more connection. Without these questions and responses, I might have assumed that I just need to work out more, that it's my spouse's responsibility to make me feel happier, or that I am depressed and I just need more things to make me feel better (which are all assumptions that I have made). Often, what we think we need never hits the mark.

Tuning In to Simplicity

Our inner child's needs are uncomplicated. Our inner child does not need a person to change everything, a new home, a career, toys, a trip, or a small number on the scale. They just need love. This simple desire may sound strange to some of us, especially if we were raised in a home where "love" was shown through commodities, vacations, or only meeting our physical needs. Our inner child's responses may seem too simple. We may still want to look for something external to "fix" our inner child. Still, we can be assured that healing comes from the intangible: the regulation of our nervous system, the ability to feel safe and secure in our bodies, words of truth and affirmation, a greater understanding of our authentic selves, and a greater connection with God, ourselves, and others.

We may also find that our inner child does not know how to respond to our questions. We may have an inner child, specifically a wounded child, who doesn't know what they want, desire, or need. We also may have a protective part who is suspicious of those who ask questions. This part of us may have learned that we must keep our cards to ourselves. We must not share anything vulnerable. The protective part believes our honest sharing will leave us used, misunderstood, or rejected. Our adult self may also be tempted to stop asking. We may think, "Well, we are not going to get anything from our inner child anyway," but the truth is, when we do not get a clear answer, our inner child needs us even more. We might have to do the first three steps—anchor, acknowledge, and attune—repeatedly before we can begin asking, but the answer is to never give up on our inner child and never stop asking.

Kaylee's Story

Kaylee is a twenty-year-old client who never learned to explore her inner world. She saw many social workers, behaviorists, and doctors, including therapists, neurologists, and cardiologists, throughout her life and was told she had everything from anxiety disorder to borderline personality disorder. During the initial stages of our work, I admit I started to wonder if maybe there was some truth to the diagnoses. Getting Kaylee to open up was difficult, let alone connect with her inner child.

At the time, Kaylee suffered from debilitating anxiety that made it difficult to get out of bed, go to school, and connect with others. When I would meet with Kaylee, she was often quiet and soft-spoken, vacillating between "I want to get better!" and "I am tired! I don't want to see you anymore!" When I would ask Kaylee just about anything, she would often respond, "I don't know."

Kaylee was severely blended with her wounded child and protective part. However, if I remained steadfast in my compassion and empathy, Kaylee would continue to attend therapy and engage in sessions. I often responded to Kaylee's nonanswers with comments like: "It is okay not to know," or "I am sure these questions get old." I then would use what I knew about her inner child to answer for her. For example, during one session, I could tell Kaylee was not responding because she was frustrated. I reflected, "I wonder if your inner child is tired of answering because, for so long, her responses were met with misunderstanding and misdiagnosis."

After I said this, Kaylee's demeanor shifted. She seemed to soften as she nodded her head in agreement. I continued to speak directly to her hurting parts instead of to her adult self. The more Kaylee felt heard and seen, the more Kaylee eventually would share more.

Over time, I went from not understanding Kaylee to seeing every part of her inner child, including the experiences that shaped her, what she fears most, what she loves most, and her hopes for her future. Now Kaylee practices extending the compassion and empathy I offered her to her inner child. When her inner child responds with "I don't know," she remains present, gives her permission not to know, and uses different ways to engage with her. During one session, Kaylee told me, "My inner child isn't really saying anything, so I told her, let's just go for a walk with the dog today and see those flowers we like." I was so proud. Kaylee's response is what it looks like to be in a relationship with our inner child and to draw near to what is hurting and afraid within us, even when we are not sure what our inner child really needs.

Befriending Work: Asking Our Inner Child

Let's practice drawing near to our parts now. Using the bilateral journaling technique we learned in the previous chapter (see example on page 129), take a moment to ask your inner child questions and then write down what you hear. The questions can be as simple as "What is your favorite movie?" or more complex like "What do you desire most?"

You can also go back to the journal exercise you completed in the last chapter and ask your inner child after you have attuned to them, "What do you need from me?" or "How can

I best support you?" Then write down their responses on the right side of your folded paper.

Ask and You Shall Receive

Too often, we give up on ourselves when we do not know how to connect with our inner child. We might have this experience when we are journaling. Oftentimes many clients will say when journaling, "I just don't know what to say," or "I am really not sure what I think or what I feel. So, what do I write about?"

When it comes to giving space to our inner voice, we must not have any expectations or judgments. We must allow it just to be what it is. Even if what we hear inside is, "This is stupid! I don't know what to write!" or "We have better things to do than this strange stuff," we make space for it. Every response we receive is valuable information that helps us to understand what child part is rising to the surface and an unmet need that may be buried deep.

There are times, however, when our inner child really does not know how to respond because a question is beyond their limited understanding. When we encounter this, we must use our anchor—our relationship with God—and ask God for help. Jesus says, "Ask, and it will be given you; seek, and you will find; knock, and it will be opened to you" (Mt 7:7).

Imagine if we approached God with this faith. Many of us have been primed not to turn to God during our small moments of need. We may have developed inner vows that get in the way of turning to God, such as "We need to be totally self-suffi-cient," "We cannot burden people," or "We need to figure it out ourselves at all times." Sometimes, our difficulty approaching God may not be about inner vows. Sometimes, it can be our adult self's misunderstanding of what it means to be a healthy and mature adult.

We must understand that healthy maturity is not about being all-knowing or never approaching our all-knowing God with our questions. Rather, it is admitting our ignorance with humility. Consider a seven-year-old child. They think they know everything. "No, that's not how you spell that!" "No, you're doing it wrong. Give it here!" "That's not how you do that dance!" As natural as this is in a child's development, as adults we have to be okay with not knowing and with turning to God for the answers. The *Catechism of the Catholic Church* states:

> The free gift of adoption requires on our part con-
> tinual conversion and *new life*. Praying to our Father
> should develop in us two fundamental dispositions:
> First, *the desire to become like him*: though created in
> his image, we are restored to his likeness by grace
> [the imago dei]; and we must respond to this grace
> [adult self].
>
> We must remember . . . and know that when we
> call God "our Father" we ought to behave as sons of
> God. . . .
>
> Second, a *humble and trusting heart* that enables us
> "to turn and become like children": for it is to "little
> children" that the Father is revealed. . . .
>
> Our Father: at this name love is aroused in us . . .
> and the confidence of obtaining what we are about to
> ask. (2784–85)

St. Thérèse of Lisieux saw herself as God's little child, and through this lens, when she was presented with just about anything, she could confidently turn to God, trusting that what she asked for, she would obtain. In her published writings in *The Story of a Soul*, she wrote, "We can never have too much confidence in the good of God. . . . As we hope in Him so shall we receive" (Lisieux 199).

We can approach God in the same way. We do not need elaborate speech, to say all the "right" words, or to try to convince God to give us what we need. We simply have to have hope that God will respond to us. As we approach God to ask him to support our inner child, we may ask questions such as these:

- "Lord, what do I do with this part of me?"
- "What does this little girl really need?"

- "I don't know how to help this part. Can you help her, Lord?"
- "Help me to see what you see in this little boy."
- "What do I do with this image of my inner child? Show me the truth."

We will hear the answers to these questions as we grow in our childlike faith. It could be through an audible voice, a person or experience, or a clear sign, but more often than not, it is through an inner wisdom budding between the confusion and the unknown.

Throughout my time doing inner child work, I have heard God say to me:

- "Give her rest."
- "Bring her to me."
- "Just be still and continue to love on her."
- "Do not worry. She's in good hands."
- "Protect her."
- "Give her a voice."

It is important to note that God's responses will always increase our love. We can trust that if the response is rooted in virtue, does not contradict truth, and fills us with consolation, it is the voice of God. If the response is fear-based or reactive, or brings more doubt and resistance to doing what we know is right, we can assume it is our protective part. Our protective part has kept us safe for so long, so sometimes, this becomes the main voice of authority in our lives, which makes it difficult to hear the voice of God or even our own Spirit-led adult self.

In this befriending work, we also may hear the voice of the enemy. The voice of the enemy typically will be accusatory. We may feel attacked instead of experiencing something within that is afraid, mistrusting, and in need of guidance. The enemy likes to play on our weaknesses and our wounded child's deepest insecurities to increase doubt, confusion, and despair. Sometimes, we may hear the enemy's voice after hearing a loving voice or having a profoundly healing experience. We may start to disbelieve that it was God's voice or that the healing experience was real. This can be another ploy of the enemy that we want to be on guard against.

Consider reviewing the lists below to explore the differences between the enemy's voice, God's voice, the voice of our inner child, and the voice of our Spirit-led adult self.

The Voice of the Enemy

- "You need to give up. There is no hope."

- "How could you really believe God would come through for you?"

- "You are not good enough for God's love. You are just a sinner, and that's all you ever will be."

- "You should just try it. What's the harm? A little bit won't hurt."

- "You are worthless!"

- "You don't need to ask for help. You got this! Everyone will just disappoint you."

- "You are all alone."

- "You don't need to follow that commandment. That one doesn't even make sense."

- "You deserve this!"

The Voice of God

- "For I know the plans I have for you . . . plans for welfare and not for evil, to give you a future and a hope" (Jer 29:11).

- "Fear not, for I am with you, be not dismayed" (Is 41:10).

- "Be of good cheer, I have overcome the world" (Jn 16:33).

- "Come to me, all who labor and are heavy laden, and I will give you rest. Take my yoke upon you, and learn from me;

for I am gentle and lowly in heart, and you will find rest for your souls" (Mt 11:28–29).

- "My grace is sufficient for you, for my power is made perfect in weakness" (2 Cor 12:9).

- "I will make all my goodness pass before you, and will proclaim before you my name 'The LORD'" (Ex 33:19).

- "For the mountains may depart and the hills be removed, but my mercy shall not depart from you, and my covenant of peace shall not be removed" (Is 54:10).

- "Peace I leave you; my peace I give to you" (Jn 14:27).

- "So you have sorrow now, but I will see you again and your hearts will rejoice, and no one will take your joy from you" (Jn 16:22).

The Voice of Our Inner Child

- "I am scared."

- "I am not enough."

- "I am just going to mess up."

- "Nobody will love me."

- "Let's just quit while we are ahead. We are going to get humiliated."

- "I am not sure if God really cares."

- "I don't know what I am good at."

- "Let's play!"

- "I need a hug. Someone hold me, please."

- "I just want to be free!"

- "I want to create!"

- "I can't do this anymore. It's just too much."

- Review the list of core beliefs in chapter 3 for how our wounded child typically sounds.

- Review the list of vows and agreements in chapter 4 for how our angry child or adolescent self sounds.

The Voice of Our Spirit-Led Adult Self

- "This isn't right."
- "We need to rethink this."
- "Let's consider our options."
- "Let's pause and pray."
- "We need to slow down."
- "Let's try that again."
- "We aren't being very compassionate."
- "What's going on?"
- "That doesn't sound like God."

- "Something isn't right here."
- "Let's look to God."
- "This is too much for us."
- "We need help."
- Review the examples of healthy vows and agreements and the gifts of the Holy Spirit in chapter 5 to get a better understanding of how the adult self sounds.

When we notice these attempts to steal our security and safety with God and the security and safety we develop with our inner child, we can use simple deliverance prayers such as "In the name of Jesus, I reject the lie of the enemy," or even in the words of Jesus, "Get behind me, Satan!" (Mk 8:33). Prayers like this help us to focus in on God's truth and prevent us from dialoguing with anything that will only bring us more suffering.

When we strengthen our relationship with God and support our protective part's healing, distinguishing the voice of God and hearing God speak will become easier. We will know when it is time to slow down, listen, and apply what we are hearing and when we can vehemently reject what we are hearing. As a rule of thumb, when we are unsure whose voice it is, but it is keeping us stuck in a place of desolation, we can just reject it. We want to enter a loving relationship with God and our inner child—not with the enemy. Therefore, we must create strong boundaries around anything that dishonors and creates division with our healthy vows and agreements.

We also might encounter God's silence in this work and may even doubt God's presence, but we should never confuse God's silence with his absence. Sometimes the silence points us to see something we are not seeing yet. The more we practice imaginary prayer, instead of hearing anything, we may see Jesus picking up our inner child, rocking our inner child back and forth, wiping our wounded child's tears, or simply listening to our protective part's rants. We can use this imagery to help us discern what our inner child may need and how the Lord might call us to respond.

Jesus tells us, "Whatever you ask in prayer, believe that you receive it, and you will" (Mk 11:24). We must receive the images, sensations, felt sense, and inner wisdom with faith. God will always communicate back to his children. He will not leave us alone with our questions and our inner child's unmet needs.

We may not like Jesus's responses, just as we may dislike our inner child's responses. I cannot tell you how many times I have told God, "Really? That's all I need to do?" But the truth is never complicated. God wants to speak to his children in a way that we will understand. All we have to do is allow ourselves to become that child again by bringing our inner child to him and learning how to listen. We must also recall that Jesus trusted in the Father because he listened to the Father. Even if that meant having to be alone in a wilderness for forty days and forty nights, Jesus knew that he had to do whatever it took to tune out all the other noises around him to hear God's true voice.

In the same way, we must also create the right conditions for ourselves to train our ears to listen to God's true voice. These right conditions may look like creating more silence in our life. We might need to take a break from podcasts, social media, and YouTube videos. We might need to go on more retreats or designate time to be alone with our thoughts. As we learn how to listen to God, we can then begin to use what we hear to respond to our inner child and deepen our love for our inner child and for God.

Araceli's Story

Araceli, a forty-four-year-old second-generation immigrant from Colombia, learned from an early age that she should never ask questions or have her own desires. Araceli's job was to be obedient and serve her immigrant parents, who needed support assimilating into American culture. Her childhood experiences shaped her to become a woman that anyone would be proud of. She was generous with her time, lived independently, served the Church, and supported her aging parents with the money she made at her job. However, what many people did not see, including her parents, was that all of the caretaking was crushing her imago dei. Araceli was living with a wounded child who was depressed, anxious, and communicating her needs through many physical health issues. As a result, Araceli could not experience her Spirit-led adult self, which made her feel insecure as an adult woman. Araceli had no idea what she wanted, felt, or needed, nor how to protect herself in a healthier way.

When I encouraged her to ask God for support and to allow God to bring internal order and to strengthen her Spirit-led adult self, she was afraid.

"I am scared to ask God for anything."

"Why, Araceli? What's coming up for you?" I asked.

"God has given me so much. I should know how to do this. I shouldn't be burdening him with my own failures."

I tried to get to the heart of what Araceli was saying. I could hear she was projecting her feelings about her parents onto God. "Araceli, I hear you're afraid. You have lived feeling like a burden to your parents for so long. Nothing you ever did felt like enough."

"Yeah!" she exclaimed. "I know I failed them. I am still failing them."

"Doesn't this sound a lot like your wounded child's core belief?" Araceli had identified that her wounded child felt like a failure, so I knew what part of her was coming up.

"Yeah, I guess you're right," she said.

"Yes, it is not your adult self. Your adult self can ask God for help. Your adult self can use her voice. She knows she is not a burden and that God wants to care for her."

"Yeah, I guess it's not my adult self who feels that way. There is a part of me that knows this to be true." Then, she looked worried again and said, "What if God doesn't respond? Or what if he does and tells me something I am not ready for?"

I nodded my head, helping her to see that it was okay to voice her worries and concerns out loud, and then gently responded, "Yes, we need to support your child parts to know that it can be safe to ask God for help and trust that he will respond with love and understanding to meet what you need right now."

Araceli's adult self was eager to begin supporting her inner child to experience this, but her child parts were weak. They were heavily burdened, afraid, and full of shame. The only way we could get Araceli to ask God what she needed and use the gifts of the Holy Spirit was to spend more time in the anchor stage. We had to help her parts feel safer. We also had to help her protective part understand that she had permission not to have everything figured out and to prioritize her needs, desires, and feelings.

Tuning In to God

We may have a similar experience to Araceli. We may need more time anchoring or developing the safety and trust that it is okay to go to God directly for support. We also may have a protective part that still projects our experiences with our parents onto God and, as a result, does not trust that God's response will be loving or supportive. Job in the Bible had similar fears and apprehensions regarding approaching God. We can imagine that his protective part led him after he experienced the trauma of losing his property and children and suffering great agony for an extended time. But then, like Bartimaeus, Job begins to see the truth and writes,

> For God speaks in one way, and in two, though man
> does not perceive it. In a dream, in a vision of the
> night, when deep sleep falls upon men, while they
> slumber on their beds, then he opens the ears of men,
> and terrifies them with warnings, that he may turn
> man aside from his deed, and cut off pride from man;
> he keeps back his soul from the Pit, his life from per-
> ishing by the sword. (33:14–18)

This faith-filled proclamation declares hope for our inner child and the parts who are suspended in our trauma, grief, sin, or attachment injuries. We want them to see who they are in relation to who God is. We want them to receive God's truth through prayer and the many ways he communicates his truth, like a balm for our soul.

We can also turn to God and receive God's truth through scripture. Scripture can help us better understand who God is and hear his voice. For "the word of God is living and active, sharper than any two-edged sword, piercing to the division of soul and spirit [our internal fracture], of joints and marrow, and discerning the thoughts and intentions of the heart" (Heb 4:12). As we read and meditate, we can notice when God is speaking to us through scripture and write it down and then speak it out loud to our inner child.

Befriending Work: Letting God Speak

Try connecting with your inner child now by going to a safe, calm place in your mind's eye and imagining God telling your inner child the following:

- "Fear not, for I am with you" (Is 41:10).

- "Behold, I make all things new" (Rv 21:5).

- "Behold, I am with you and will keep you wherever you go" (Gn 28:15).

- "In everything [I work] for good with those who love [me]" (Rom 8:28).

- "[I] will wipe away every tear from [your] eyes" (Rv 21:4).

- "I have called you by name, you are mine" (Is 43:1).

Now, try asking God questions and listening to God's voice. Take your journal out again, using the bilateral journaling technique from chapter 8. Label the left side "God" or another name for God that makes sense to you, and label the right side "adult self." Then ask God anything in your heart right now, and write those questions on the right side. Wait until you hear a response, then write it down on the left side. Continue to ask questions if you need God to clarify. The exercise is complete when you feel you have asked what you need to ask for now and received at least one response.

Ultimately, we want to better understand God's will for our inner child and what we need to heal. We need to uncover how to be in a healthy relationship with our inner selves and make critical decisions to protect and care for them. The truth is, every part of us wants to believe God loves us and will take care of us because we are made by God and for the glory of God. However, we will have to calm ourselves enough to support our parts to reclaim that truth, and then we can act on it. We can begin taking the information we receive from them and respond as God would.

Through this step in our befriending, we get closer to the heart of our inner child. We uncover what they still need from us and discover new ways to meet that need in our adult lives. As a result, we get one step closer to our healing and wholeness.

Prayer

Father, I want to understand better what my inner child needs and what you desire for my healing. Give me the graces I need to ask the right questions and vulnerably share the parts of me that are coming up with you. Give me the graces I need to hear the truth and respond to that truth with love. Amen.

10

Act

I was in a heated conversation with my spouse when suddenly I felt my body stiffen in panic. My heart began to anxiously pound, and I could hear the voice of my inner child in my mind, yelling past my husband's words.

"I am not enough! I can't do this! This is too much!" became the mantra deafening all other noise. My husband continued, not recognizing the internal army that just declared war in my head. I could feel myself wanting to run and hide, kick and scream, but all I could do was stand there, frozen with frustration and muted by my protective part's growing hopelessness. My inner child was present, and my Spirit-led adult self was losing her anchor.

I then closed my eyes and allowed myself to escape from my perilous plight into fight-flight-freeze-fawn. I took a deep breath, called on the Holy Spirit, and then mentally told my inner child, "I see you. I hear your fear. I feel your anxiety. I am right here." Suddenly, my body shifted. I felt a release. In a moment when I was beginning to feel the weight of my wounds and my protective part's inability to protect me from the increasing stress, I was not alone. I was not abandoned. I had accessed God through the Holy Spirit, drew near to my inner poverty, and befriended my inner child.

This is my hope for you, dear reader. You have been on a journey to discover and draw near to your inner child so that in moments of confusion, darkness, sudden shifts, high stress, strong emotions, and loud and pestering thoughts, you are not alone. You have a father in God and a friend in you. You can access the Holy Spirit alive in you. You can utilize the resources that help you remain rooted in your anchor and the newfound knowledge of your inner child and no longer abandon yourself.

Our Legacy of Healing

Every time we choose to be present to our inner world, notice the shifts in our emotions and body, listen intently to the different noises in our mind, and find the voice of God at the center of it all, we are befriending our inner child. We are giving ourselves and future generations new opportunities for greater connection, security, safety, and hope, and we are breaking generational cycles of trauma, toxic shame, dysfunction, and sin. We are participating in God's redemptive love and leaving a legacy of healing.

Therefore, in *act*, the last *A* in this five-step process of befriending our inner child, we become active cycle breakers. We commit to consistently breaking down what binds us and steals our power to live in the image and likeness of God so that we can become all we are called to be.

As we consistently befriend our inner child and respond to their needs with love, our child parts shift. Our wounded child lets go of their harmful core beliefs. Their qualities, such as sadness or oversensitivity, can become more neutralized and aid in the softening of our hearts. Feelings like powerlessness or anxiety can become connective and deepen our bonds with others and with God. Core beliefs like "I am not enough" and "I am all alone" can become old beliefs from the past that can strengthen and aid in our adoption of new, healthier beliefs about ourselves.

When our protective part begins to see that our wounded child's needs are being met, this part of us will slowly begin surrendering their control and learning healthier ways to adapt. The protective part may still seek self-protection, but it won't be in a way that hinders or harms us. Instead they can help us to be attentive and intentional. This part's anger and mistrust can even be the catalyst for further change and self-growth. There is nothing that we can discover within ourselves that cannot be healed, integrated, and befriended.

I often imagine our work as shepherding sheep and leaving the ninety-nine to go after the one. When one of our parts begins to move away from the flock, we go after the lost one and bring them back to where they belong. It does not matter if the part doesn't seem all that important or we know that they might eventually come back on their own; we recognize the value of every part of us, and out of love, we respond. We allow ourselves to slow down, draw near, and recover the sheep that have lost their shepherd.

Just as Jesus and the Father are one (see John 17:21), every part of us is invited to be a part of the flock and experience oneness. As we seek to practice and experience this reality, we can use another acronym, A.C.T.I.O.N.S., because it will take a lot of conscious actions to experience the inner oneness we need. We must remember that these A.C.T.I.O.N.S. can be a road map to help us along the way and aid our befriending, but ultimately, what we are acting on is whatever our inner child reveals to us or what God directs us to do. Our persistence, responsiveness, and trust in God, ultimately, are what elicit the change.

A.C.T.I.O.N.S.

Let's explore the actions we must complete to respond to our inner child and experience inner and outer oneness.

Affirming

As we befriend our inner child, we must constantly affirm and reaffirm their goodness. When we are triggered, dysregulated, or experience relational conflicts and stress, our wounded child's core beliefs, feelings, and traumatic memories will bubble up to the surface. We may have thought that we grew past those beliefs or memories and no longer experience those distressing feelings, but our wounded child will still occasionally doubt, fear, or become insecure. They may struggle with the validity of the healthier beliefs we have adopted, especially if someone shares something that seems contrary to our newfound self-knowledge or we have an experience that leaves us feeling powerless, ashamed, or inadequate.

Therefore, ongoing "actions" include reminding our fractured parts of the truth of who we are. We must respond lovingly to their ambivalence and speak words of blessing and affirmation:

- "You are God's beloved."

- "You are capable of accomplishing great things!"

- "Fear not; God is with you!"

- "You are special in God's sight."

Each time we affirm the goodness of our inner child, we help them to rest in their imago dei and strengthen the connection with ourselves, God, and others. We can stay more rooted in our anchor and, as a result, can work through any triggers and doubts with more reassurance and peace.

Correcting

Our protective part will want to take over often. For a large portion of our lives, this part has been in leadership, especially if we are survivors of complex or developmental trauma. We will have to be vigilant to see when this part of us is coming up. When we are quick to respond or make a choice, feel our anger rise, dissociate, judge ourselves or others harshly, or when we are too hypervigilant and defensive, we can be assured that it is most likely our protective part trying to be in charge again to protect us from perceived harm.

Correction should never be harsh, abusive, or overly critical. When our correction is rooted in love, it should sound firm, be explicitly clear, and offer a strong reminder of our healthy vows and agreements. Here are some examples:

- "I know you are trying to protect me right now, but responding in that way will only hurt us more."

- "We cannot talk like that! That's unacceptable. We have made a commitment to live with integrity."

- "We are allowed to be angry, but we are not allowed to lash out like that!"

Sometimes, we may think that being compassionate means never calling ourselves or others out. We may think it means only speaking kind and affirming words, but true compassion not only suffers with but seeks to prevent suffering. Our protective part isn't always aware that their responses can cause more suffering. Therefore, we must gently step in to help this part honor our internal boundaries, restrain impulses, and respond in a more gentle way.

We might even have to correct our inner child's internalizations. For example, we may hear a small voice that says, "I am just so anxious!" or "I am so lazy!" In order to get to the heart of our inner child and help them see the deeper truth, we may gently say, "We are not anxious, we are just afraid of being rejected. We are not an anxious person but a person who wants to be accepted," or "We are not lazy. We are growing in self-discipline. We are still working on our fears of failure but we are not a lazy person." Our ability to help our inner child in real time when their interpretation is faulty will help move them from accepting the lie to embracing God's truth.

Training

As we continue to learn and grow and allow the Spirit-led adult self to lead, we must train our fractured parts to become more integrated with our imago dei and Spirit-led adult self. All of the saints eventually became professional trainers. They used their faith and the gifts of the Holy Spirit to train for what they knew to be true. Through their practice and persistence, they all eventually experienced oneness within themselves and with God. In the same way, we must constantly train to become more of a Spirit-led adult self and train our inner child how to live as a whole child of God. This training can look like:

- Forming new neural pathways through repetition and focused attention on our inner world.

- Remembering our new, healthy inner vows, agreements, and core beliefs and using them during times of distress.

- Practicing virtue and living with integrity.

- Responding consistently to our inner child each time we notice their presence.

- Regulating our emotions and using what we know about our inner child to make connections to the past.

- Regulating our nervous system through various regulation strategies and the befriending work we completed in this book.

- Living with dual awareness, the "both/and," so that we are not quick to catastrophize, assume, or give up.

- Setting and honoring boundaries over and over again.

Our training will sometimes feel exhausting, especially when we are just beginning this process of befriending, but over time, it will get easier. It will become more natural and habitual. Just as it was natural to respond from a fractured child part, it will be natural to respond from our Spirit-led adult self.

Intuiting

When we go through the steps of anchoring, acknowledging, and attuning, we may not need to ask our inner child anything. We may already know what they need. When we befriend our inner child, we get to know our inner child deeply. We know their fears, desires, unmet needs, hopes, insecurities, and blind spots. We can therefore use this knowledge to promptly intuit what our inner child needs fairly quickly.

When my children were infants, I relied on my intuition a lot. My children could not speak and tell me what they needed, but as I learned each child's temperament, cries, body language, and facial expressions, I could begin to intuit what they needed: food, a diaper change, connection, soothing, and so on. Our inner child is the same. Their needs do not change much. Once we know them, we can use all the cues and our awareness to meet their needs.

Our intuition will also increase when we establish more safety in our bodies and security in God. As we befriend our inner child, we become more aware of our gut instinct. We become better stewards of our bodies. We know when something is off and what our inner child will need to rest in the ventral vagal state and remain rooted in their belovedness.

Obeying

When we hear the word *obey*, many of us often feel uncomfortable. Obedience can be confused with stripping away our power. Obedience can sound like a threat to our true self, a self that we have already lost and are in the process of recovering. However, obedience is at the heart of accomplishing God's will and becoming who we are created to be.

Obedience is about trusting in God's goodness. When children are truly obedient, they are trusting in an adult's leadership. Even if they do not feel like doing something, they learn to do it over time. There is security that gives them the inner freedom to move through their emotions and trust in authority. We see this poignantly in Jesus's ministry. Jesus knew who he was (Jesus had security) and what he was called to do (God's leadership was present), and he completely trusted in God's will (Jesus had safety with God). Through this secure and safe relationship with God, he could lay down his life and work through the human feelings that came with his suffering and impending death. Ultimately, Jesus was able to complete his God-given mission, aligning his intellect, will, and divinity to act accordingly and transform death. As a result, Jesus was resurrected into full glory, and through Jesus's obedience, he pleased his heavenly Father greatly.

This Gospel truth is essential to highlight because being a mature and healthy adult does not mean doing whatever we want; instead, it means being obedient to God's will. It means learning how to lay down our life and experience resurrection daily out of love for God. In our daily dying and rising, death begins to lose its sting. The darkness does not overcome us. The light of our imago dei becomes more and more radiant, our safety and security expand, and our true self is recovered.

Nurturing

Our inner child will always need nurture. God has wired us to need a nurturing other in order to be all we are created to be.

So, our actions must be rooted in nurture. We may sometimes think that this means always responding with a soft tone, arms ready to comfort, and a gentle demeanor, but always responding this way would be perfection, something we cannot always attain ourselves.

We already have a perfect parent who is capable of nurturing us perfectly: God. Therefore, we do not need our perfection or anyone else's perfection. However, what we did need when we were children and still need to this day to nurture well is repair.

Repair is the ability to respond to our imperfections and the imperfection of others with humility. It means saying, "I am sorry," and reconciling over and over again, no matter how uncomfortable or tiring it gets. Imagine how different our lives would be if people offered repair after they harmed us. How nurtured we would feel!

Fortunately, we do not need anyone to offer us repair now as adults to heal our inner child. It would be nice and helpful, but it isn't necessary. We are the ones who can offer repair to our inner child. We can do this in the following ways:

- Apologize when we abandon or fail to lead our inner child.

- Take ownership of our sins and receive God's mercy in the Sacrament of Reconciliation.

- Let our inner child know that we see them when they feel triggered, and help them make sense of their feelings.

As we repair, we strengthen our nurture. Our hearts remain open and responsive, and our weaknesses and vulnerability increase our ability to offer compassion, connection, and deep attunement to ourselves and others.

Serving

The last and final of the A.C.T.I.O.N.S. that we will have to practice in our befriending is service. As we work to model our adult selves more and more after Jesus, we will have to become more comfortable with service. For those of us who were parentified or who have lived codependent, this may sound like an easy thing to do. Parentified children and codependents are constantly serving. However, our service must move from a wounded place to a place of freedom and honor of our imago dei.

As we see in the story of Martha and Mary, Martha thought she was serving Jesus well, but Jesus told her that Mary had chosen the better way. Jesus is not concerned with us serving for the sake of pleasing others, earning worth, or being dutiful; rather, Jesus wants our service to be authentic love. When Mary served, she sat at Jesus's feet and listened to his words. This is also the same Mary who falls at Jesus's feet and wipes and anoints them (Jn 12:3). The service Jesus applauds and exemplifies is one of slowing down to recognize and honor the presence of God. When we serve our inner child and the inner child in others, we ultimately are recognizing and honoring the presence of God. We are imitating Jesus who, taking on our humanity, also wiped and anointed our feet (Jn 13:1–17) and listened intently to our words, including our questions, fears, doubts, and our desires.

Imitating Jesus is often much easier to do with others than it is when we are alone with our own selves. It can be hard and even strange to imagine serving our own selves in this way. We may have concerns or judgments that we will become too selfish or too self-seeking, but when it comes to serving our inner child, the service we provide opens us up to serve God and others better. It rarely stays and ends with us. When we serve our inner child well, when we continuously acknowledge their presence and their dignity as children of God, attune to their suffering, ask what they need, and seek to get those needs met, we become a more authentic and whole person who has capacity to serve others better. The irony is that in our befriending of our inner child, we move from the childish tendency to make everything about ourselves to seeing a world in need of our befriending and a God who is all-deserving of our love and praise, and it is here radical transformation and healing occurs.

Befriending Work: Bringing It All Together

Now let's bring it all together. In part 1, we learned about each part of ourselves and the importance of befriending these parts. In part 2, we have learned about all the practical tools we will need, including the A.C.T.I.O.N.S. to help us befriend our inner child. When befriending our inner child in real time, we will want to remember these different tools and go through the five *A*'s mentally or through bilateral journaling. Let's practice now.

Beginning with *anchor*, connect with your mind, body, and spirit. When you feel grounded, then *acknowledge* your inner child. You can say or write, "How are you feeling?" Or if you can identify an emotion, thought, or behavior that may be connected to your inner child, you can say or write what you are noticing.

adult	inner child
I know that's how you felt all of your life. It hurts to know that I'm doing the same thing to you. You deserve to be paid attention to and supported.	Yeah! I don't know.
I know my words probably feel pretty empty and it's okay not to know. I am sure you don't really know what it feels like to be truly paid attention to and supported, and I am so sorry.	Thank you! You see me

Then wait to hear a response within. Next, you will *attune* by validating the emotions of your inner child. Again, wait to hear a response.

Continue responding with nurture until your inner child feels heard and seen.

Then, *ask* your inner child, "What do you need from me, or how can I best support you right now?" Once you receive a response, then commit to *act* on it.

Consider the example in the image to see what a dialogue typically looks like.

You will notice in this example that my protective part came out right away. You can see her hopelessness and fear, as well as how heavily burdened and alone she has been feeling under all the pressure to protect. Notice that I stay with her feelings. There is nothing too little or too much she can say that prevents me from acknowledging, attuning, and then asking how I can better support her. If my protective part did not know what she needed to feel better supported, I would then ask Jesus what she needs and write down what he suggests. I'd then ask my protective part if it would be okay to try Jesus's suggestion.

It is helpful to try this exercise when we notice our inner child come up or when we know that our inner child may come up. Perhaps we know that certain people, experiences, topics, or activities may trigger our inner child. We can use this tool before the trigger to regulate our inner child and perhaps even desensitize our inner child from the trigger.

We can also use this tool with others. When someone is displaying an intense emotion or sharing thoughts and beliefs that seem to be the voice of their inner child, we can begin with getting ourselves anchored, acknowledging their feelings and thoughts, attuning to their emotions, asking questions to gain clarity and to see how we can best support, and then acting on what they share with us.

We can also use this tool with God. When we are not in an anchored place to befriend our inner child or the inner child in others, we can seek God, let him anchor us, and then think about how God would acknowledge and attune to us, what he might be asking of us, and then practice acting on whatever he shares with us.

Befriending Work: Praying with Our Inner Child

Another way we can bring all the tools and A.C.T.I.O.N.S. together is through our daily prayer. Simply including our inner child in our prayer can help us connect with our innermost thoughts and feelings and bring them to God.

Listen to the audio recording on the Ave
Maria Press website of prayers for your inner
child and follow along with a free download
of those prayers by scanning the QR code here
or going to avemariapress.com/befriend-
ing-inner-child-meditations. Try imagining
yourself with Jesus and your inner child. Consider even writing your own prayer that is tailored to your
unique child parts.

Living in the Family of God

Our daily response to the invitation to befriend our inner
child thus becomes the most important work of our lives. It is
an everyday movement toward healing and wholeness. Our
affirming, correcting, training, intuiting, obedience, nurturing,
and service changes everything. It ushers us back to the family of God so that we can become one with God, and it keeps
us grounded in Christ's promise that he will never abandon
us; Christ will be with us always until the end of the age (see
Matthew 28:20).

And yet, as we remain in the family of God and hold on to
Christ's promises, we also remain very human. We come to find
that all our intentional actions never quite seem to bring us the
results we hope for. Something still feels unsettled, unresolved,
and unhealed. We may even be tempted to think we are not
as connected to self, God, and others as we thought. We were
disillusioned and perhaps even regressing.

But the only illusion is believing that we can eradicate our
humanity. As we move forward in our befriending, we will
get discouraged. We will still experience our internal fracture
from time to time. We will feel a rush of emotion and want to
respond in an old, familiar way. When this happens, we cannot
be discouraged. The goal was never about getting to a place
where we never experience human limitations and emotions,
but about discovering a way to be loved in it.

We must trust that the good work that the Lord began in
us will be brought to completion (see Philippians 1:6). As we

anchor ourselves in Christ; acknowledge what part of us is coming up and our feelings, beliefs, wounds, and the ways we may be protecting ourselves from those wounds; attune to those feelings; ask what our inner child may need; and act in response to those needs, we are simply cooperating with God's grace.

The *Catechism of the Catholic Church* states, "The ultimate end of the whole divine economy is the entry of God's creatures into the perfect unity of the Blessed Trinity" (260). When we befriend our inner child, we reflect our triune God, and God provides the final actions. God provides the graces we need, moves through our being and creates order, meets our unmet needs through his continuous love and mercy, and stitches us back together part by part.

We may not always see this, but it is happening. St. Paul writes in his Letter to the Colossians, "In him all the fulness of God was pleased to dwell, and through him to reconcile to himself all things, whether on earth or in heaven, making peace by the blood of his cross" (1:19–20). Therefore, we can trust that the Lord will reconcile everything in us. There is nothing that will be wasted. Everything that we have experienced, the injustices that never should have happened, every feeling we have held on to, every negative thought we internalized, and all the ways we have protected ourselves will be healed and integrated to mirror our loving God.

Here, our primal fear of abandonment is redeemed. We recognize the family of God is with us and will remain with us. We are united internally with our inner child and externally with our loving God, and as a result, we no longer psychologically abandon ourselves. We bring every part of ourselves to our heavenly Father, including what is unfinished and incomplete within us, and then spiritually entrust ourselves to God's providence and care.

Our Joy Will Be Complete

It is in God, through God, and with God, and in harmony with our inner child, that our joy will be complete. We will feel fulfilled and at peace, safe, and secure. We will be "of the same mind, having the same love, being in full accord and of one mind" (Phil 2:2). Who we are will never be the same, and we will bear much fruit in our adaptation and integration.

For some of us, this is a scary thought. Change can be incredibly scary. We do not want to lose any more of ourselves. We might think, *Does this mean I won't be fiery? Or quirky? Will I have to be too docile? Quiet? Forfeit some of my curiosity or ambition?*

We may have lived with our internal fracture for so long that it can feel alarming to no longer experience our woundedness and, in the process, give up aspects of our personality that we have always known. We may have become so identified with our pain or self-protection that joy, peace, security, and safety can even feel threatening.

As children growing up with complex trauma, we may have found that joy, peace, and security were often short-lived. We may have thought we could rest and receive them, but then something terrible happened. We may have also unconsciously normalized chaos. We may have learned to survive in dysfunction—constant noise, busyness, and disorder. We may get excited by the thrill and appreciate the chase. As a result, the thought of resting and living as God's beloved child may not sound too enthralling for our protective part.

As valid as our feelings are, we are not made for woundedness or for maintaining a fractured and disintegrated state. We are made for wholeness. Therefore, we can assure our protective part that living as God's beloved child is the greatest adventure. As we go on this adventure, every part of us matters and won't be bulldozed by the positive change. We can honor how our child parts have brought us to this point, as well as their unique characteristics, and we can reassure our wounded child and protective part that positive feelings and a healthy life can be safe, and even thrilling!

Joy, along with peace, safety, and security, is ours, and we will continue to grow, heal, and become all that we are created to be even in the presence of fear. Nobody can take this away from us. There are no unwelcomed thoughts, no distressing feelings, and no amount of suffering in the world powerful enough to steal what God has already won for us. So, as we befriend our inner child and live as God's beloved child, only good awaits us. All will be well, and all will be complete.

Let this be our invitation to giggle like a child. Dance like nobody's watching. Lift our arms high in surrender. Cry with fearless abandon. Experience bliss in the rain. Jump in puddles. Bravely leap, soar to new heights, and confidently say:

> I know who I am.
> I am free.
> I am loved.
> I am God's child.
> And every part of me is worth befriending.

Prayer

Father, thank you for taking me on this journey with my inner child. Thank you for inviting me and my inner child into perfect unity with your Blessed Trinity. I see the Father you are, and I see your whole child whom I am becoming. Bless my daily actions to befriend my inner child, and complete the good work you have started in me. May my joy, healing, and wholeness be complete in you. Amen.

Bibliography

Ainsworth, Mary D. S. *Patterns of Attachment: A Psychological Study of the Strange Situation.* N.p.: Lawrence Erlbaum Associates, 1978.

Anderson, Susan. *The Journey from Abandonment to Healing: Revised and Updated: Surviving through and Recovering from the Five Stages That Accompany the Loss of Love.* New York: Penguin, 2014.

Beck, Aaron T., and David A. Clark. *Cognitive Therapy of Anxiety Disorders: Science and Practice.* New York: Guilford Press, 2011.

Bradshaw, John. *Healing the Shame That Binds You: Recovery Classics Edition.* Deerfield Beach, FL: Health Communications, Inc., 2005.

Brown, Brené. *The Gifts of Imperfection: 10th Anniversary Edition.* Center City, MN: Hazelden, 2020.

Capacchione, Lucia. *Recovery of Your Inner Child: The Highly Acclaimed Method for Liberating Your Inner Self.* Introduction by Charles Whitfield. Chicago: Touchstone, 1991.

Gardiner, Cerith. "Try Mother Teresa's 5-Second Prayer to Mary for When You Need Support." *Aleteia*, December 13, 2020. https://aleteia.org/2020/12/13/try-mother-teresas-5-second-prayer-to-mary-for-when-you-need-support/.

Gibson, Lindsay C. *Adult Children of Emotionally Immature Parents: How to Heal from Distant, Rejecting, or Self-Involved Parents.* Oakland, CA: New Harbinger, 2015.

John Paul II. "Homily in Puebla de Los Angeles (Mexico)." The Holy See. January 28, 1979. https://www.vatican.va/

content/john-paul-ii/en/homilies/1979/documents/
hf_jp-ii_hom_19790128_messico-puebla-seminario.html.

John Paul II, and Philokalia Books. *Theology of the Body in Simple Language*. Scotts Valley, CA: CreateSpace Independent Publishing Platform, 2009.

Jung, C. G. *Development of Personality*. Edited by R. F. Hull and Gerhard Adler. Translated by Gerhard Adler and R. F. Hull. Volume 17 of *Collected Works of C. G. Jung*. Princeton: Princeton University Press, 1981.

Jung, C. G. *Psychology and Alchemy*. Princeton, NJ: Princeton University Press, 1980.

Lisieux, Thérèse. *The Story of a Soul: The Autobiography of St. Thérèse of Lisieux*. Edited by Agnes of Jesus. Translated by Michael Day. Charlotte, NC: TAN Classics, 2010.

Maier, Steven, and Martin Seligman. "Learned Helplessness at Fifty: Insights from Neuroscience." *Psychological Review* 123, no. 4 (July 2016): 349–67.

Nouwen, Henri J. M. *Life of the Beloved: Spiritual Living in a Secular World*. New York: Crossroad, 2002.

Paul, Margaret. *Inner Bonding: Becoming a Loving Adult to Your Inner Child*. New York: HarperCollins, 1992.

Paul VI. *Gaudium et spes*. The Holy See. December 7, 1965. https://www.vatican.va/archive/hist_councils/ii_vatican_council/documents/vat-ii_const_19651207_gaudium-et-spes_en.html.

Porges, Stephen W. *The Polyvagal Theory: Neurophysiological Foundations of Emotions, Attachment, Communication, and Self-Regulation*. New York: W. W. Norton, 2011.

Ratzinger, Joseph. *Introduction to Christianity*. San Francisco: Ignatius Press, 2004.

Richo, David. *How to Be an Adult: A Handbook on Psychological and Spiritual Integration*. Mahwah, NJ: Paulist Press, 1991.

Schuchts, Bob. *Be Healed: A Guide to Encountering the Powerful Love of Jesus in Your Life*. Notre Dame, IN: Ave Maria Press, 2014.

Schwartz, Richard C. *No Bad Parts: Healing Trauma and Restoring Wholeness with the Internal Family Systems Model*. Boulder, CO: Sounds True Publishing, 2021.

Siegel, Daniel J. *Aware: The Science and Practice of Presence—The Groundbreaking Meditation Practice.* New York: Penguin, 2020.

Siegel, Daniel J., and Tina P. Bryson. *The Whole-Brain Child: 12 Revolutionary Strategies to Nurture Your Child's Developing Mind.* Delacorte Press, 2011.

"St. Margaret Mary Alacoque." n.d. Sacred Heart Apostolate. Accessed July 5, 2023. https://sacredheartapostolate.com/devotion/st-margaret-mary-alacoque/.

Taylor, Shelley. "Tend and Befriend Theory." In *Handbook of Theories of Social Psychology,* edited by P. A. M. Van Lange, A. W. Kruglanski, and E. T. Higgins, 32–49. Thousand Oaks, CA: Sage, 2012.

Venditti, Sabrina, Lorenda Verdone, Anna Reale, Valerio Vetriani, Michaela Caserta, and Michelle Zampieri. "Molecules of Silence: Effects of Meditation on Gene Expression and Epigenetics." *Frontiers in Psychology* 11, no. 1767 (August 2020). https://pubmed.ncbi.nlm.nih.gov/32849047/.

"What Is Ignatian Spirituality?" Ignatian Spirituality. Loyola Press. Accessed July 12, 2023. https://www.ignatianspirituality.com/what-is-ignatian-spirituality/.

Whitfield, Charles L. *Healing the Child Within: Discovery and Recovery for Adult Children of Dysfunctional Families (Recovery Classics Edition).* Deerfield Beach, FL: Health Communications, 1987.

Whitfield, Charles. Introduction to *Recovery of Your Inner Child: The Highly Acclaimed Method for Liberating Your Inner Self* by Lucia Capacchione. Chicago: Touchstone, 1991.

Brya Hanan is a Catholic licensed marriage and family therapist and certified family trauma specialist who owns Hanan Hope and Healing, a private practice in Arizona.

In 2014, Hanan earned her bachelor's degree in sociology with a minor in Catholic studies at Loyola Marymount University. She earned a master's degree in counseling psychology from Holy Names University in 2017. Hanan creates webinars and workbooks to help people befriend their inner child and experience holistic healing.

She is the author of *God Whispered Gently,* a children's book she wrote about her own inner child.

www.bryahananlmft.com
Instagram: @bryahananlmft

Want help praying through your inner child healing?

Follow along with Brya Hanan
as she guides you through an audio meditation
for each of the child parts, which include:

- Adult Self Meditation
- Angry Child Meditation
- Imago Dei Meditation
- Wounded Child Meditation

Enjoy a bonus audio recording from Brya with prayers for your inner child and follow
along with a free download of those prayers from our website.

To listen, scan here or visit
avemariapress.com/befriending-inner-child-meditation